Mindful Patterns

ADULT COLORING BOOK

This Book Belongs To:

____

Disclaimer

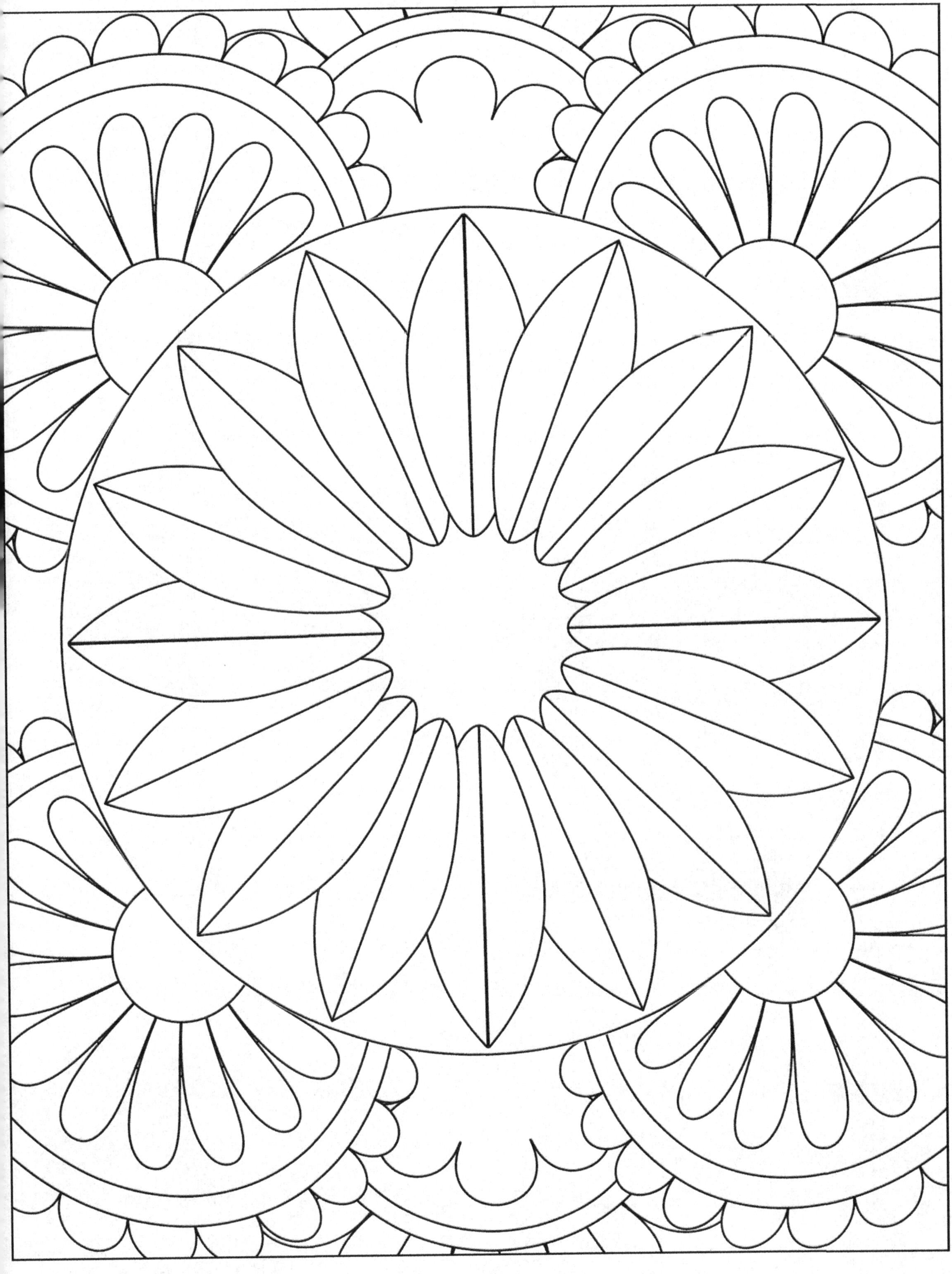

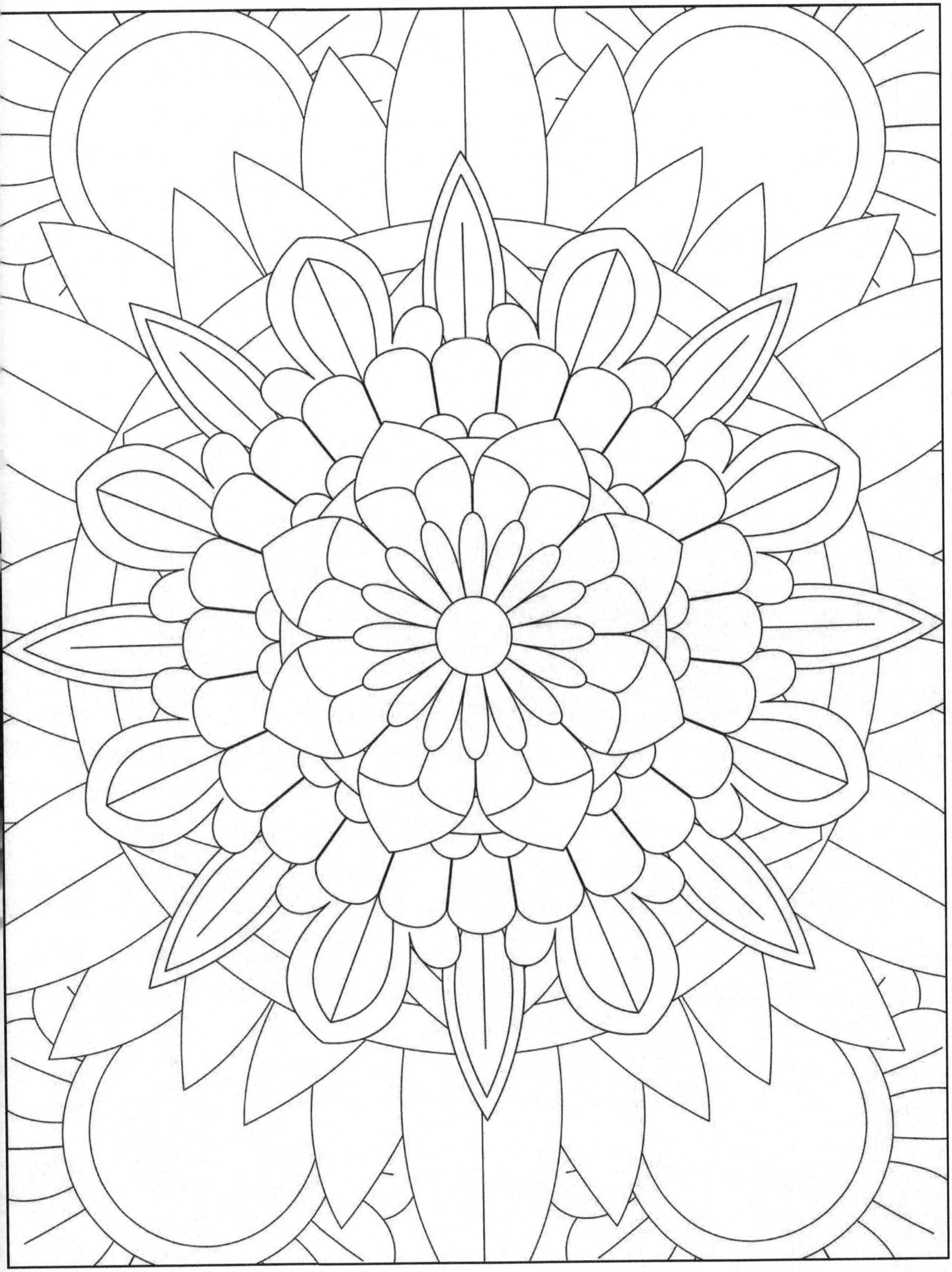

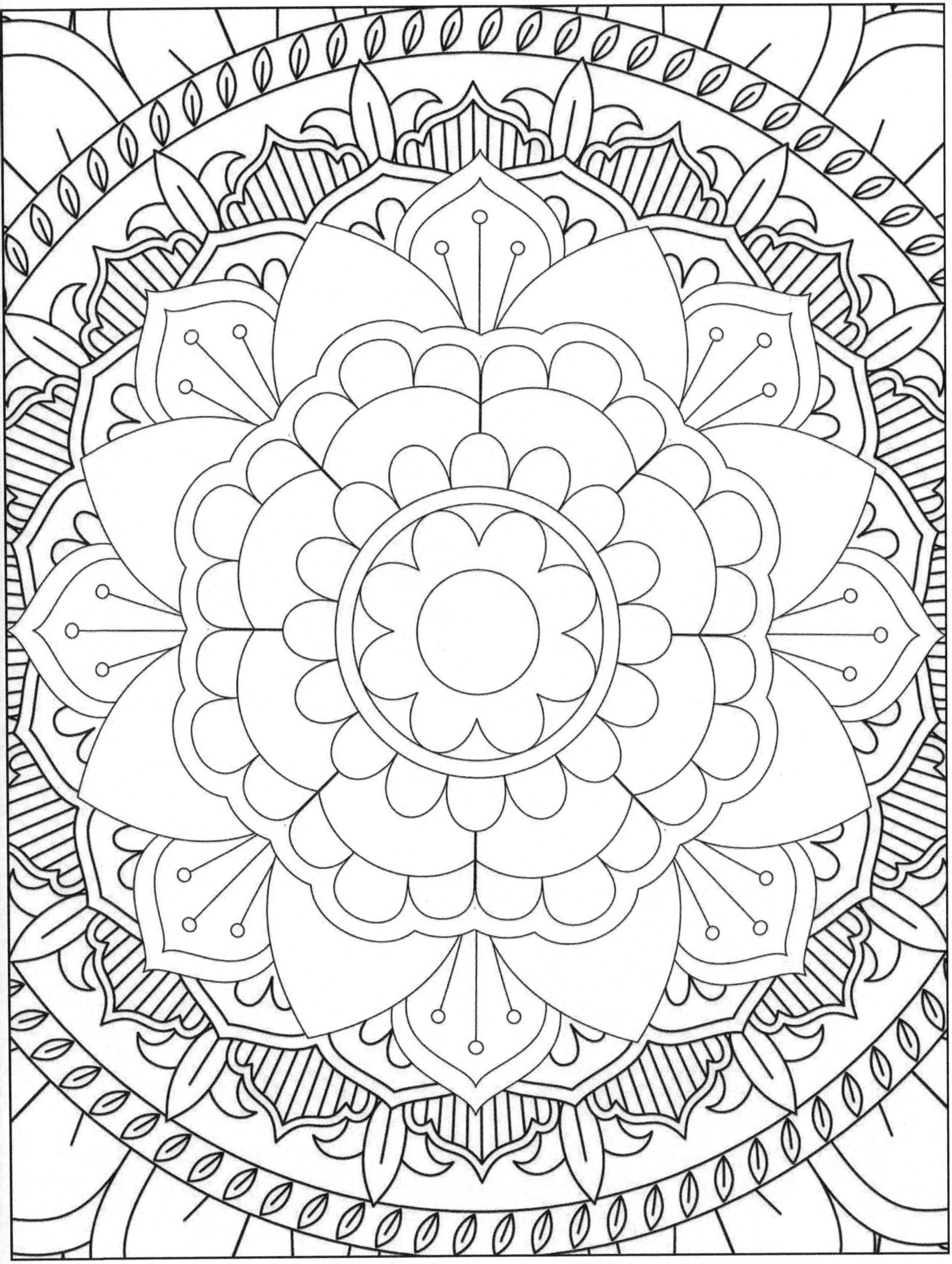

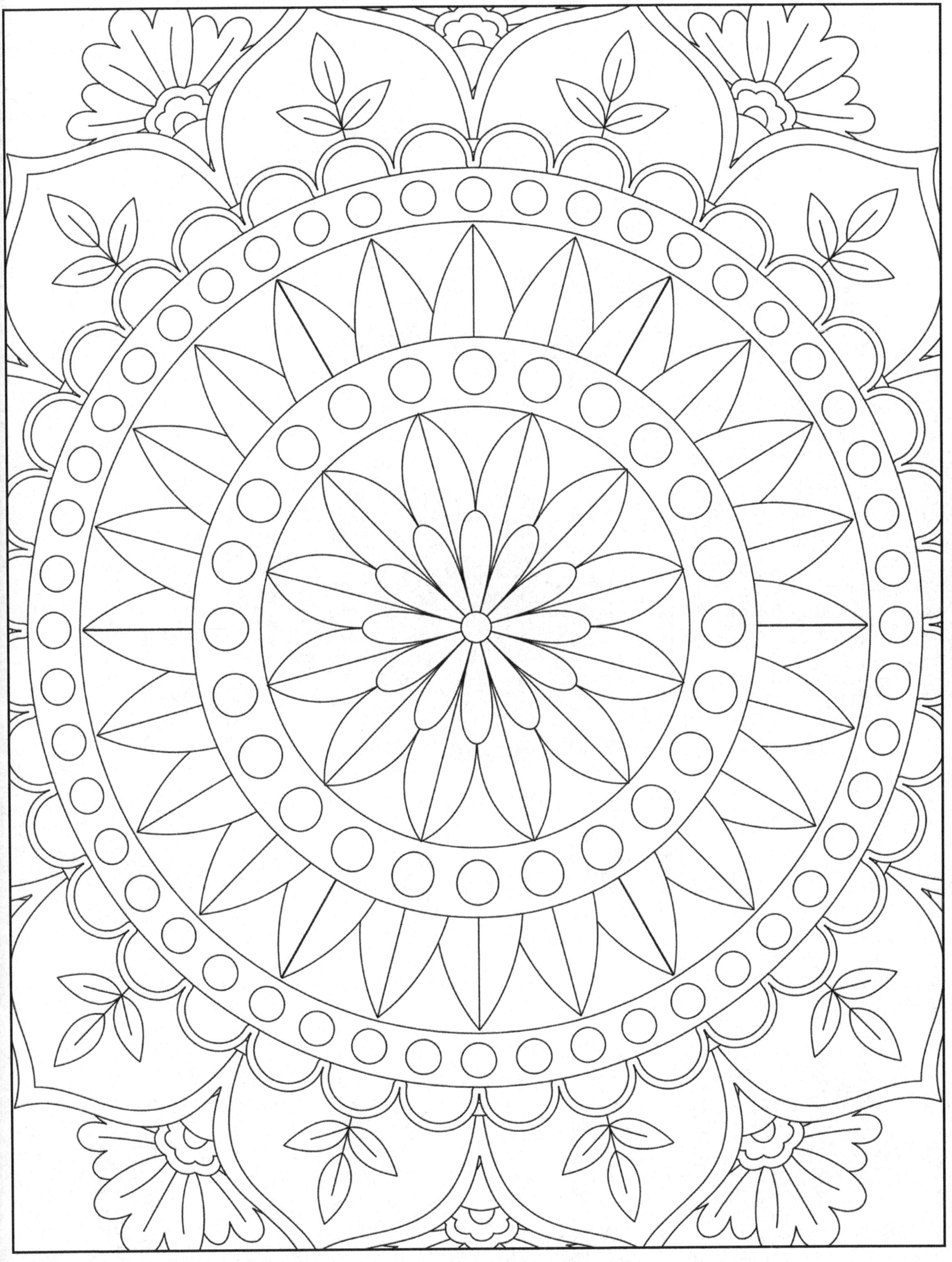

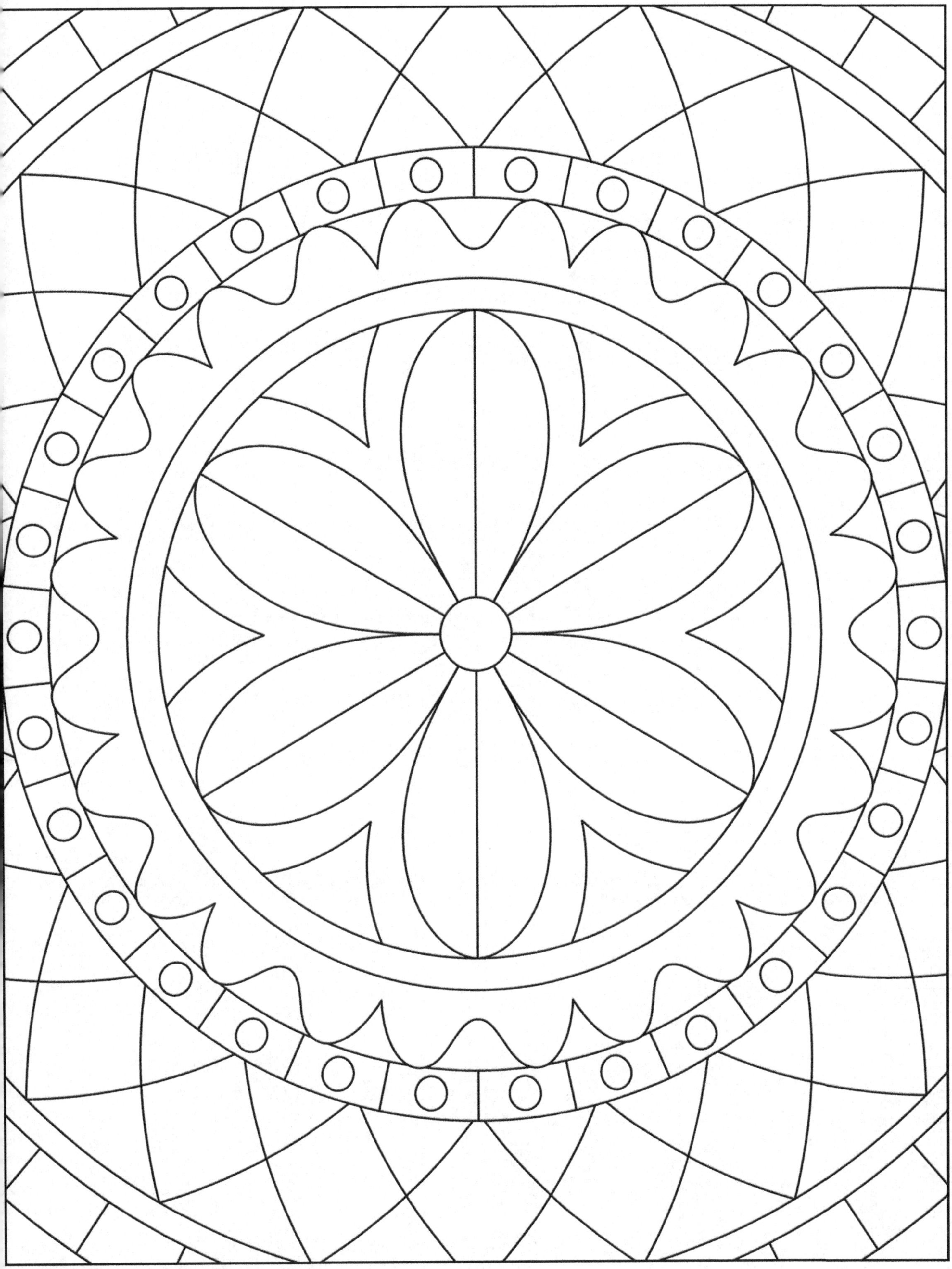

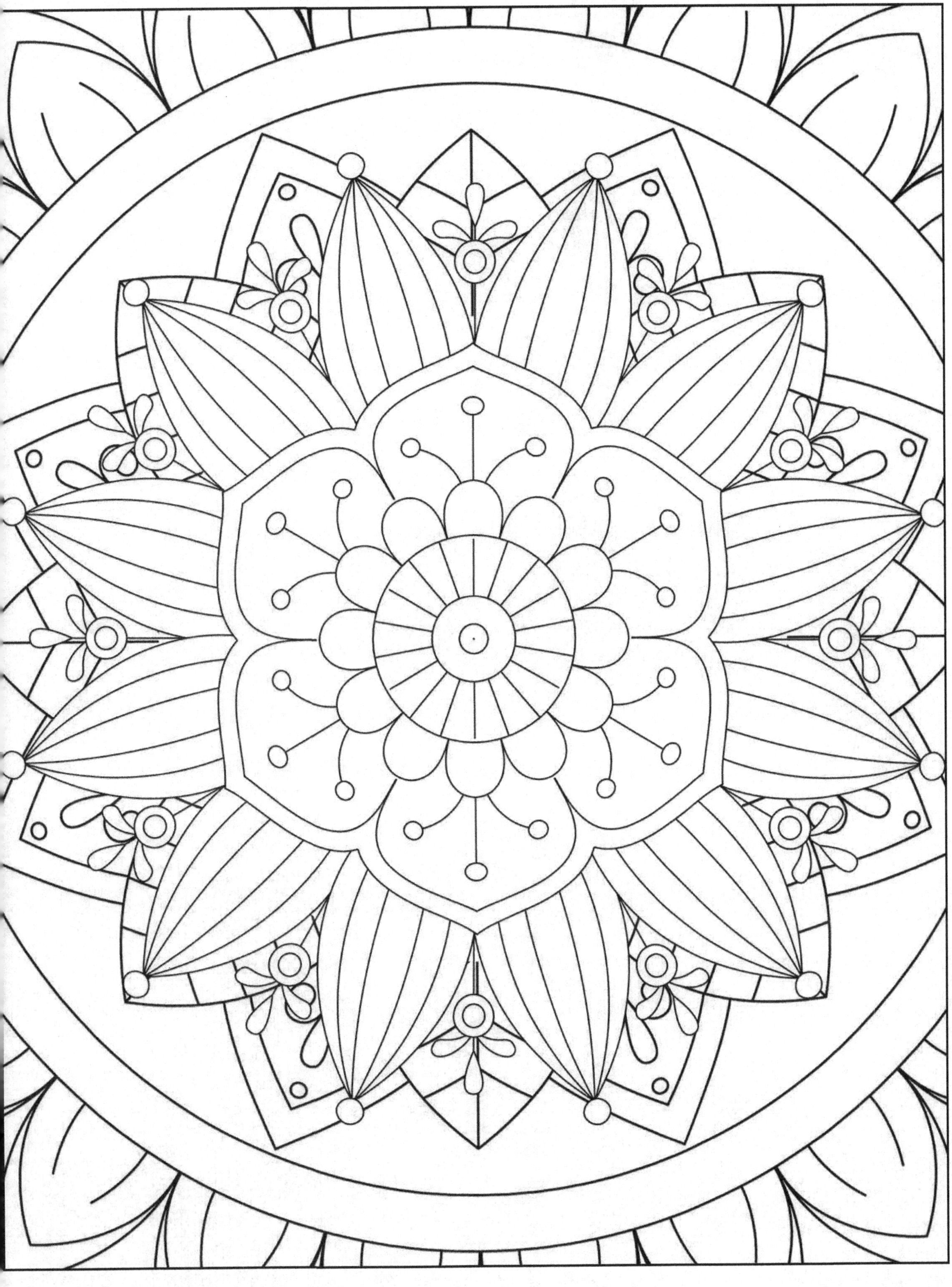

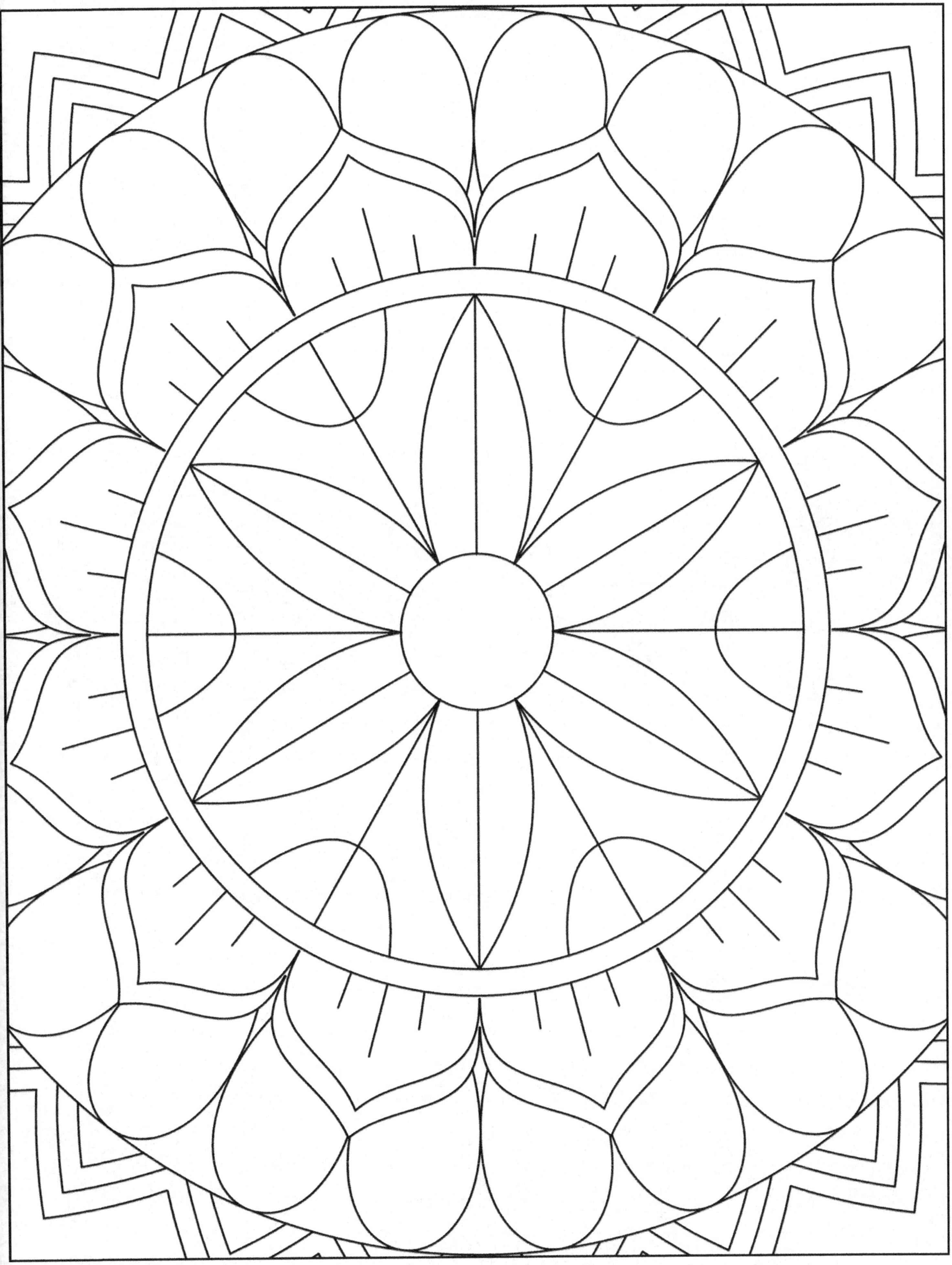

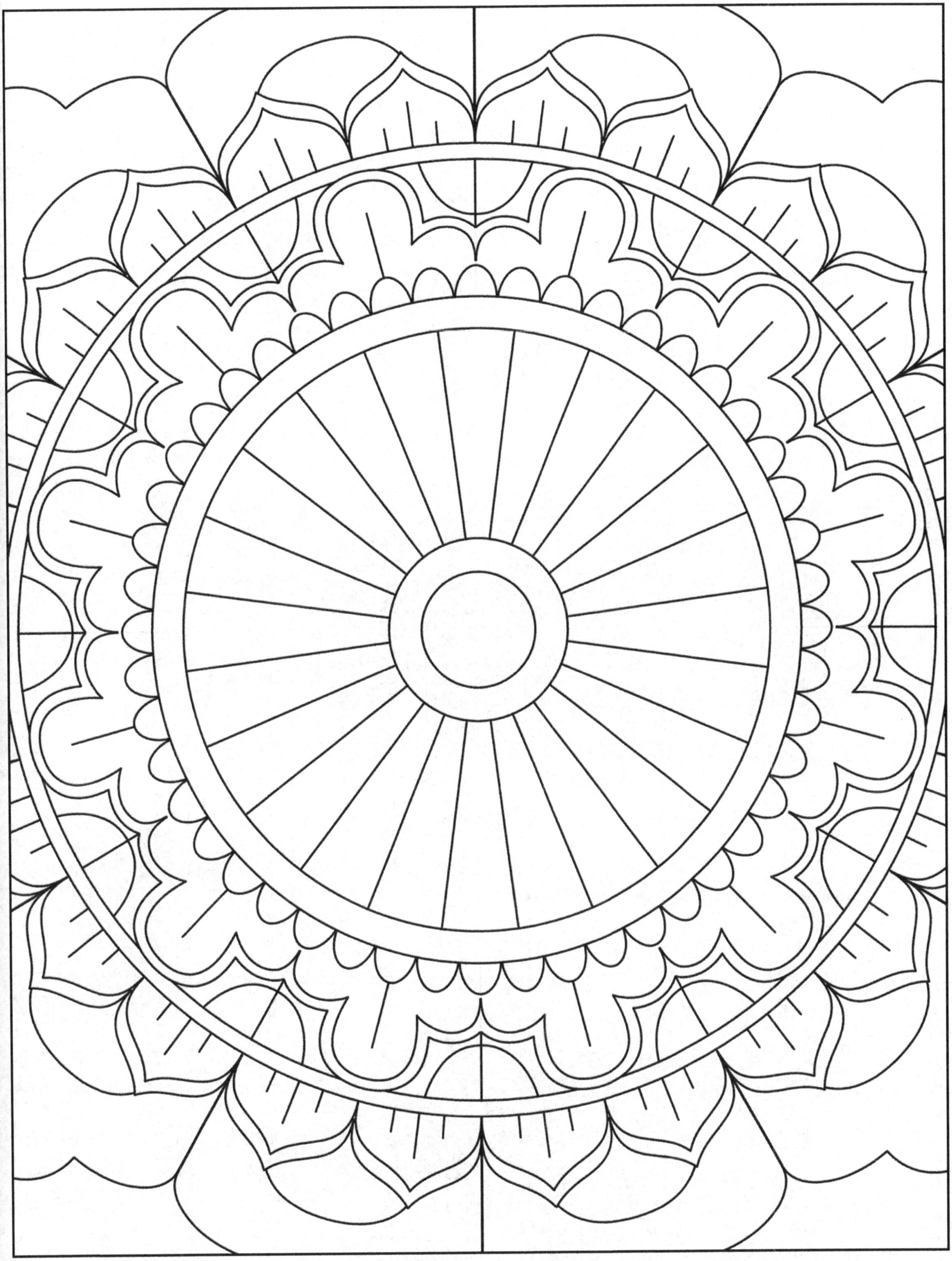

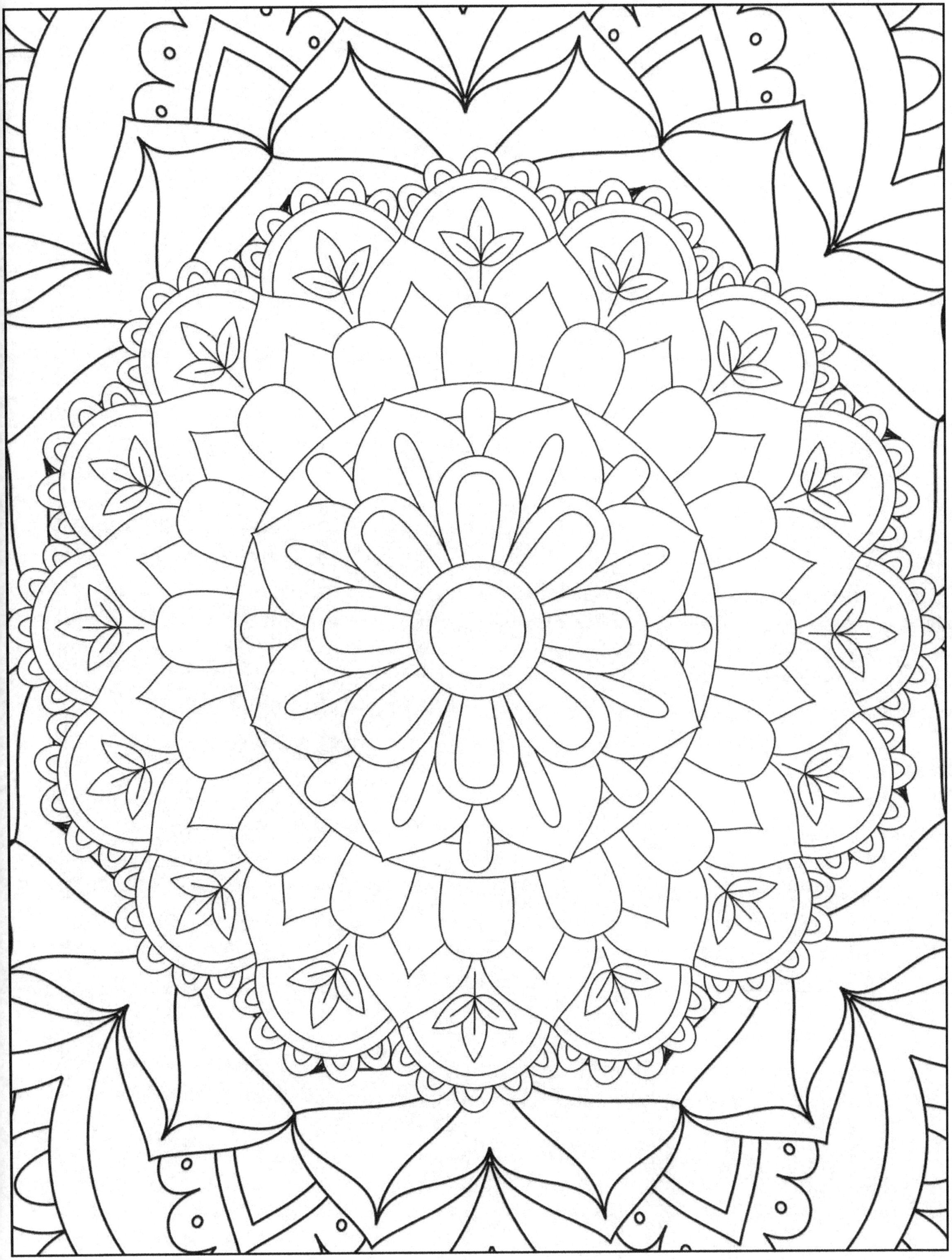

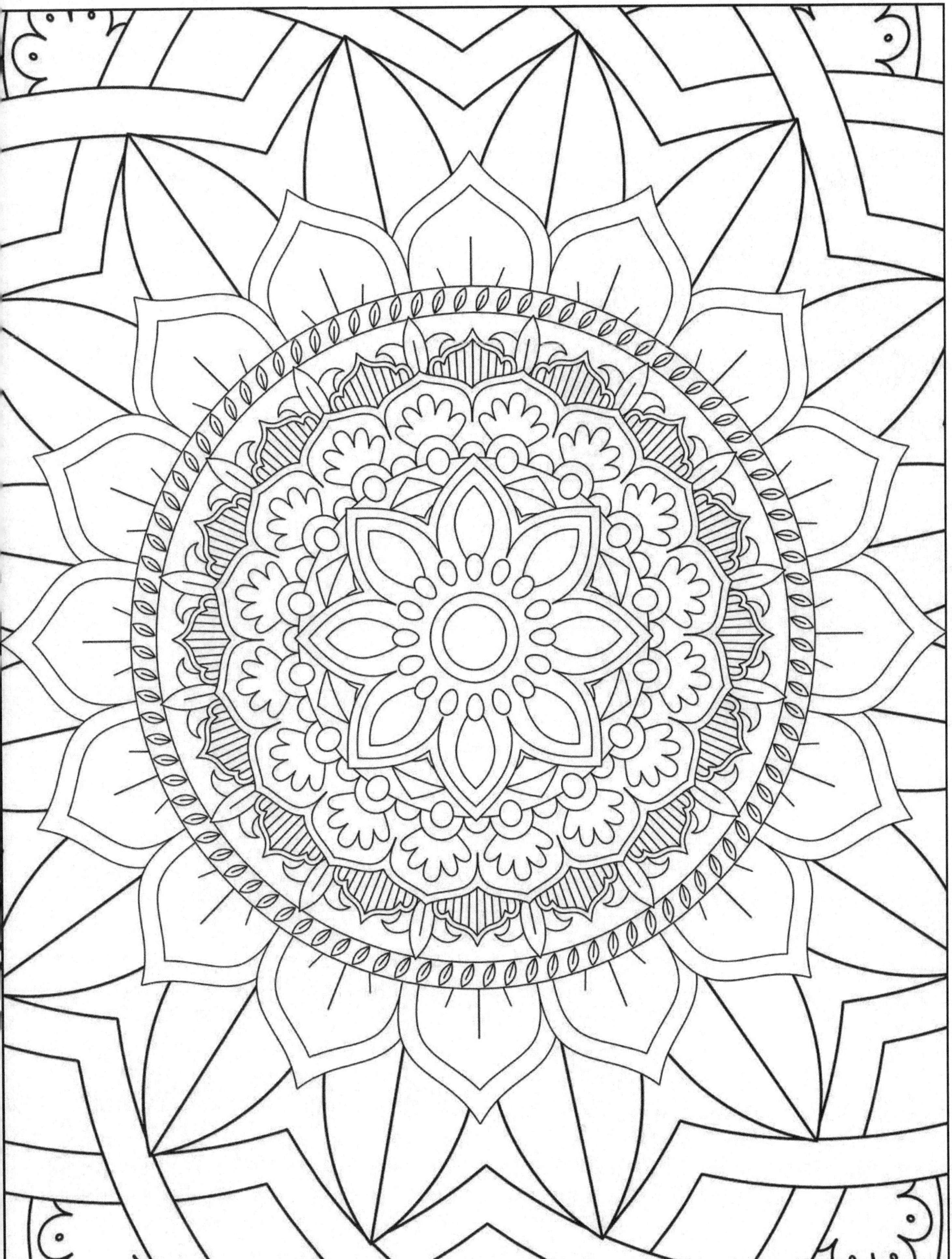

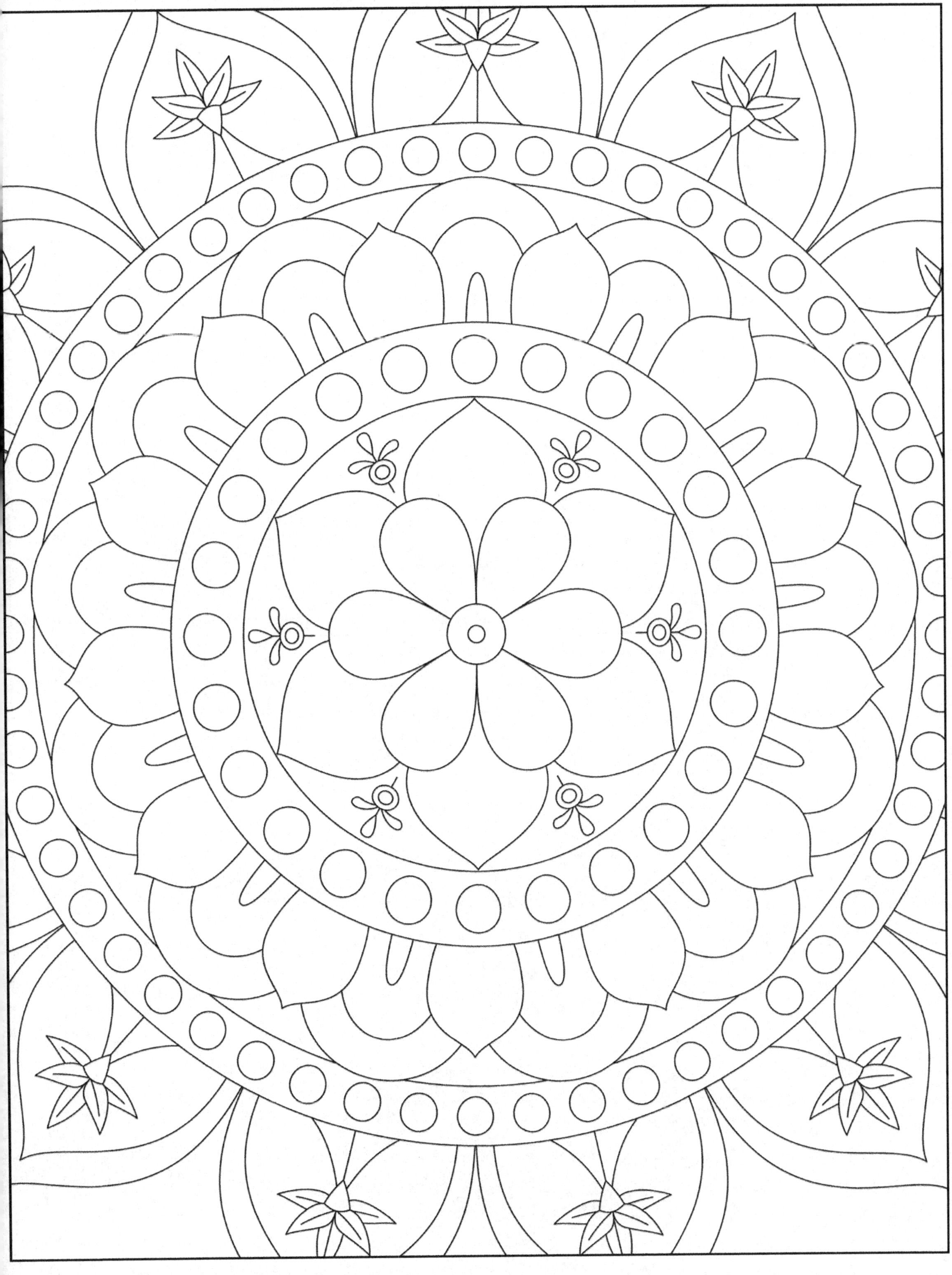

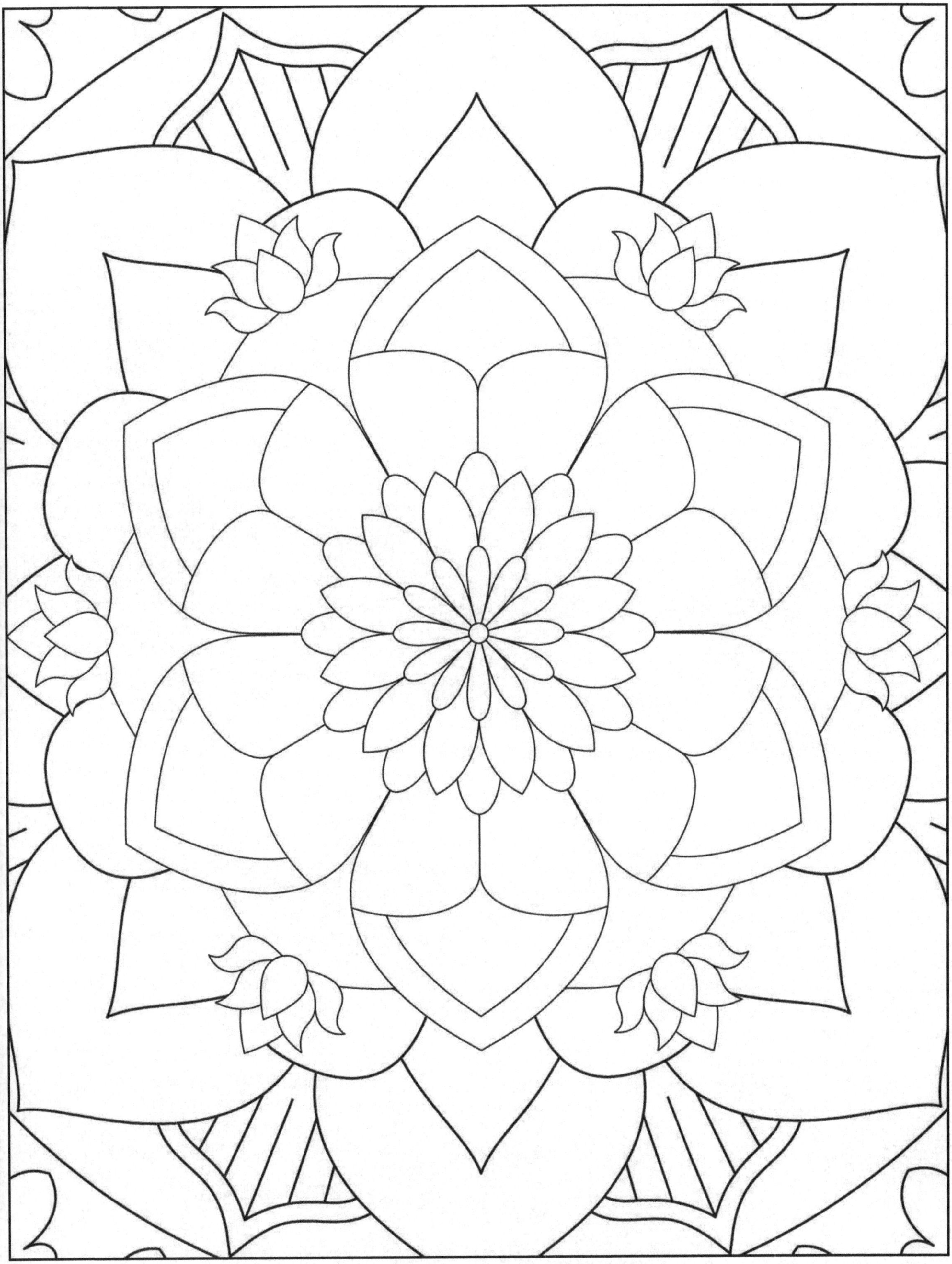

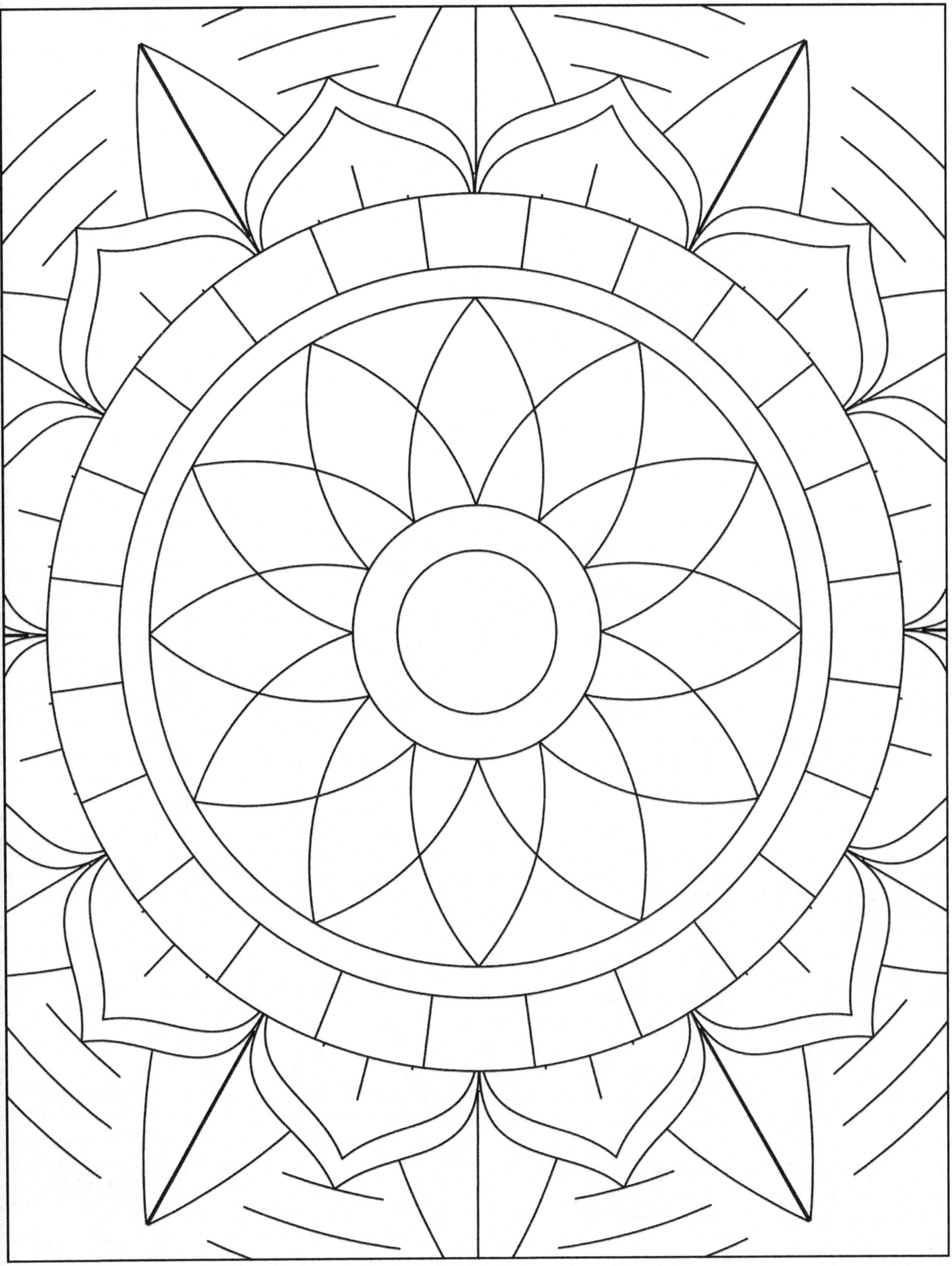

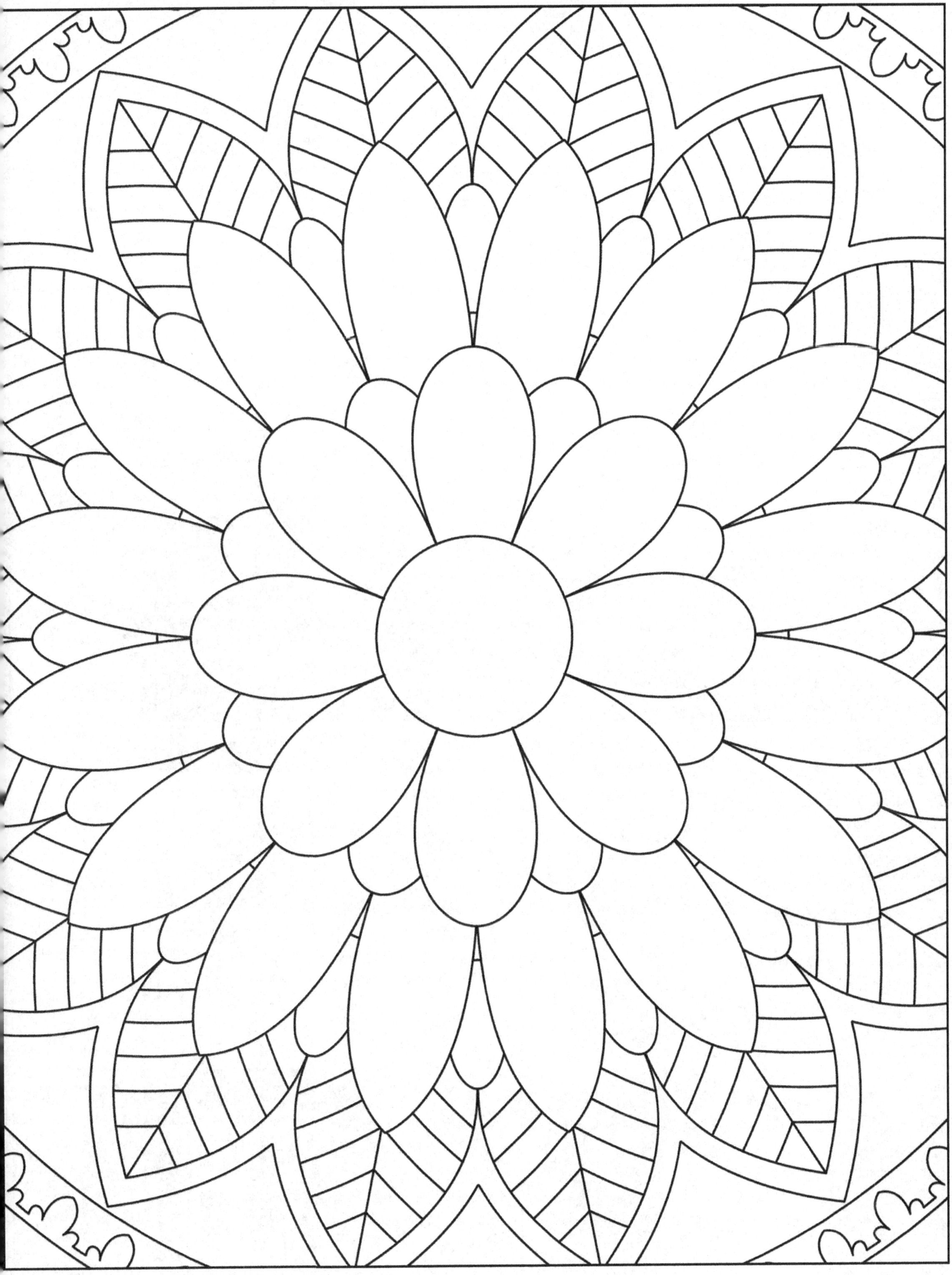

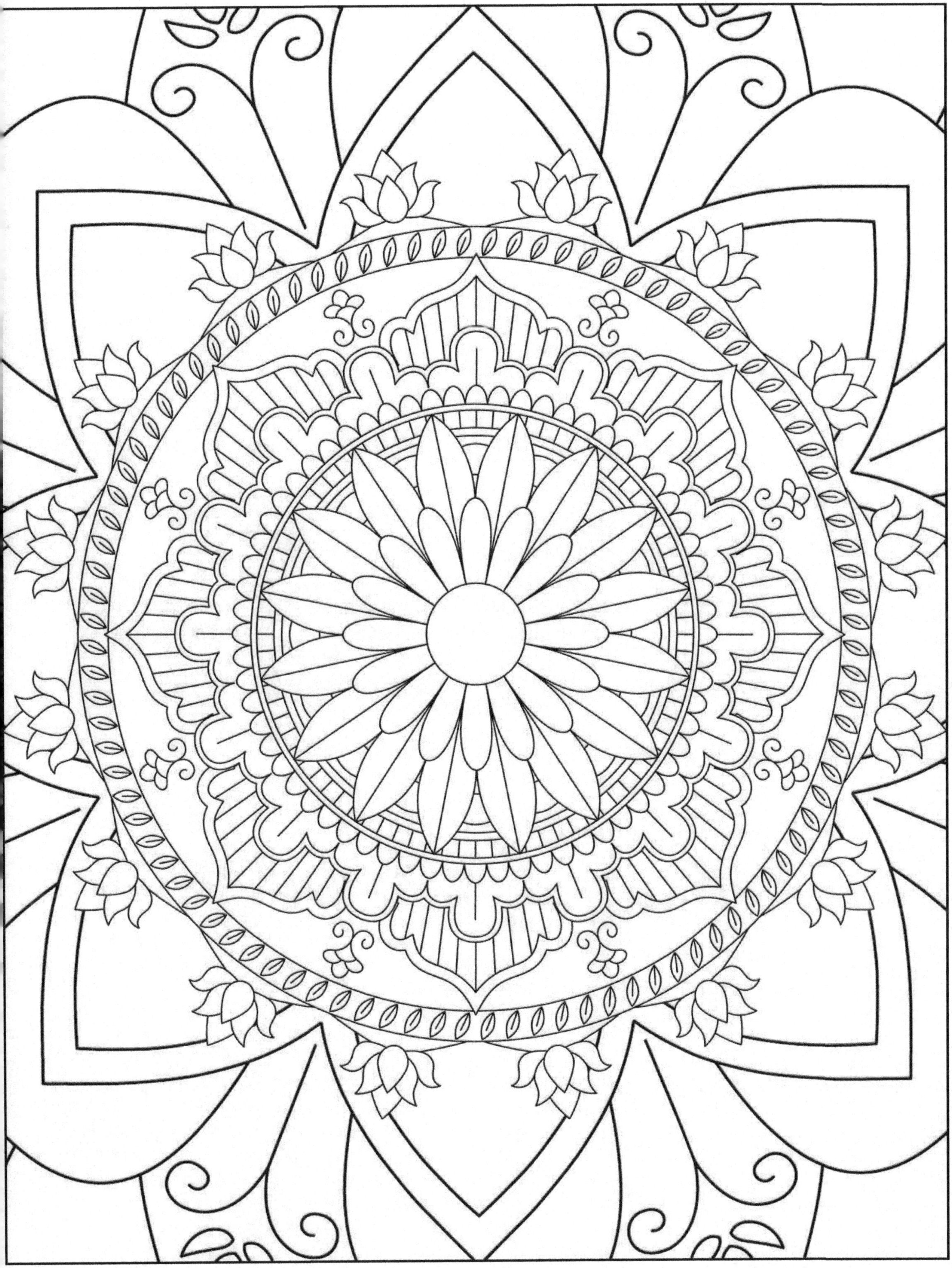

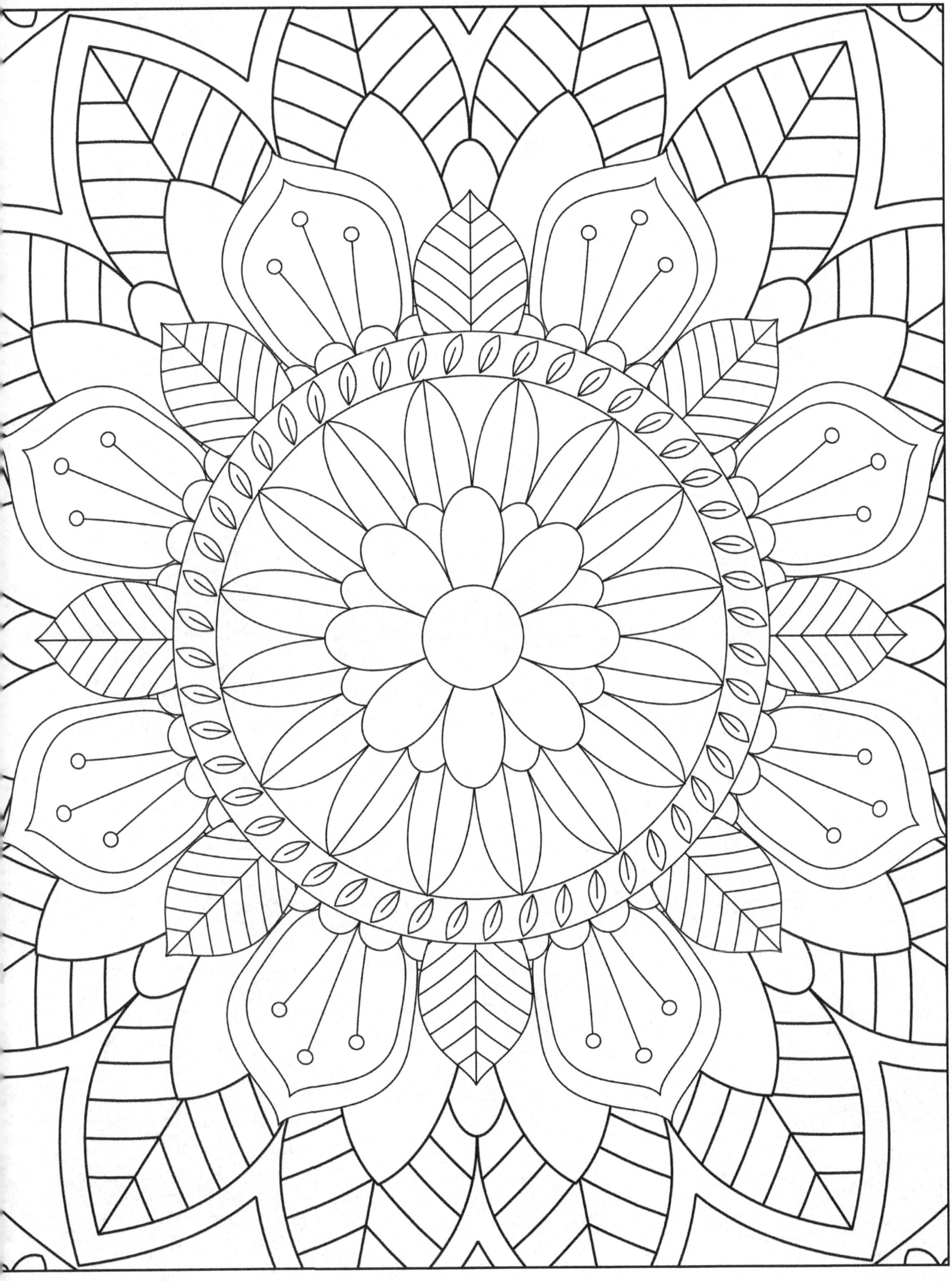

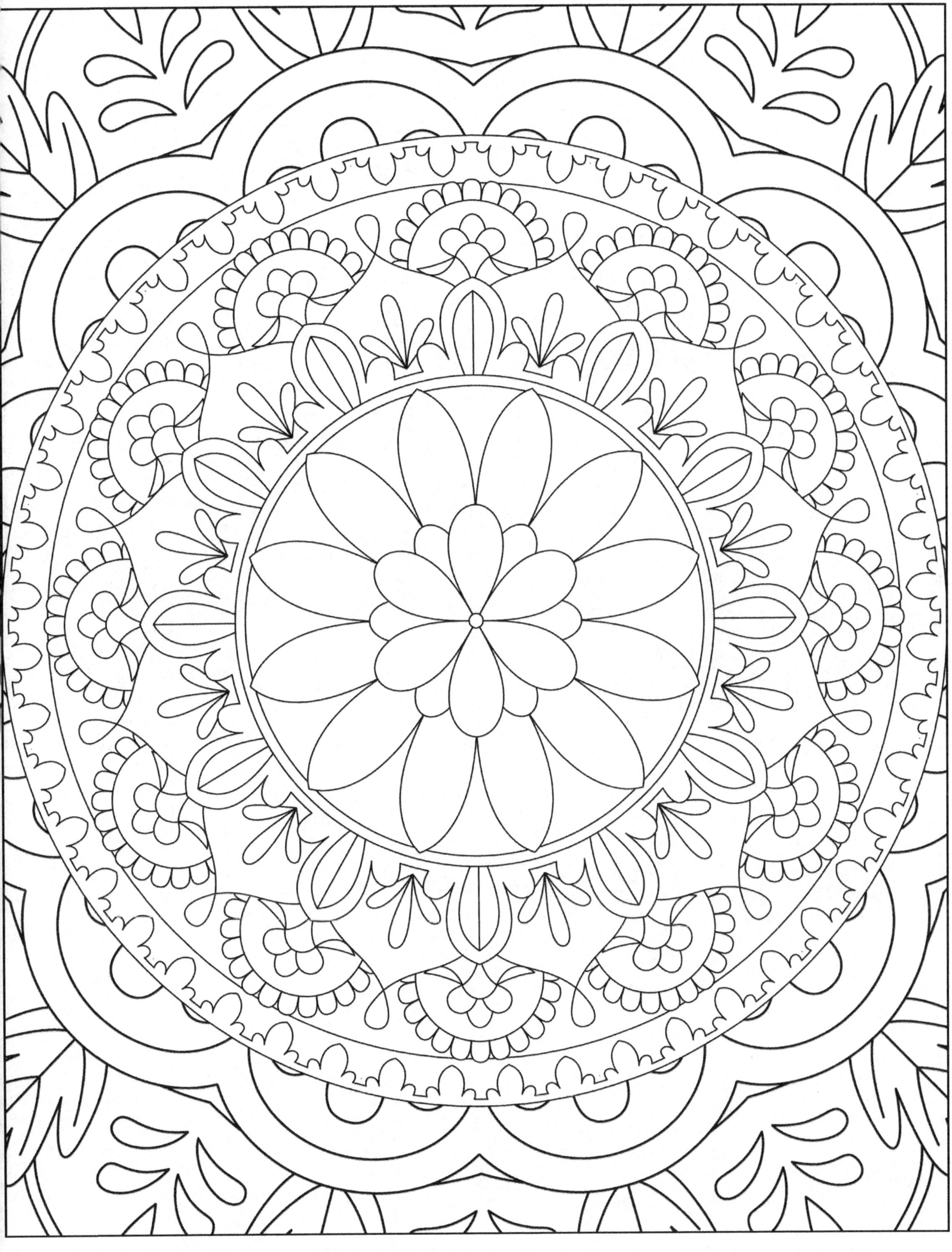

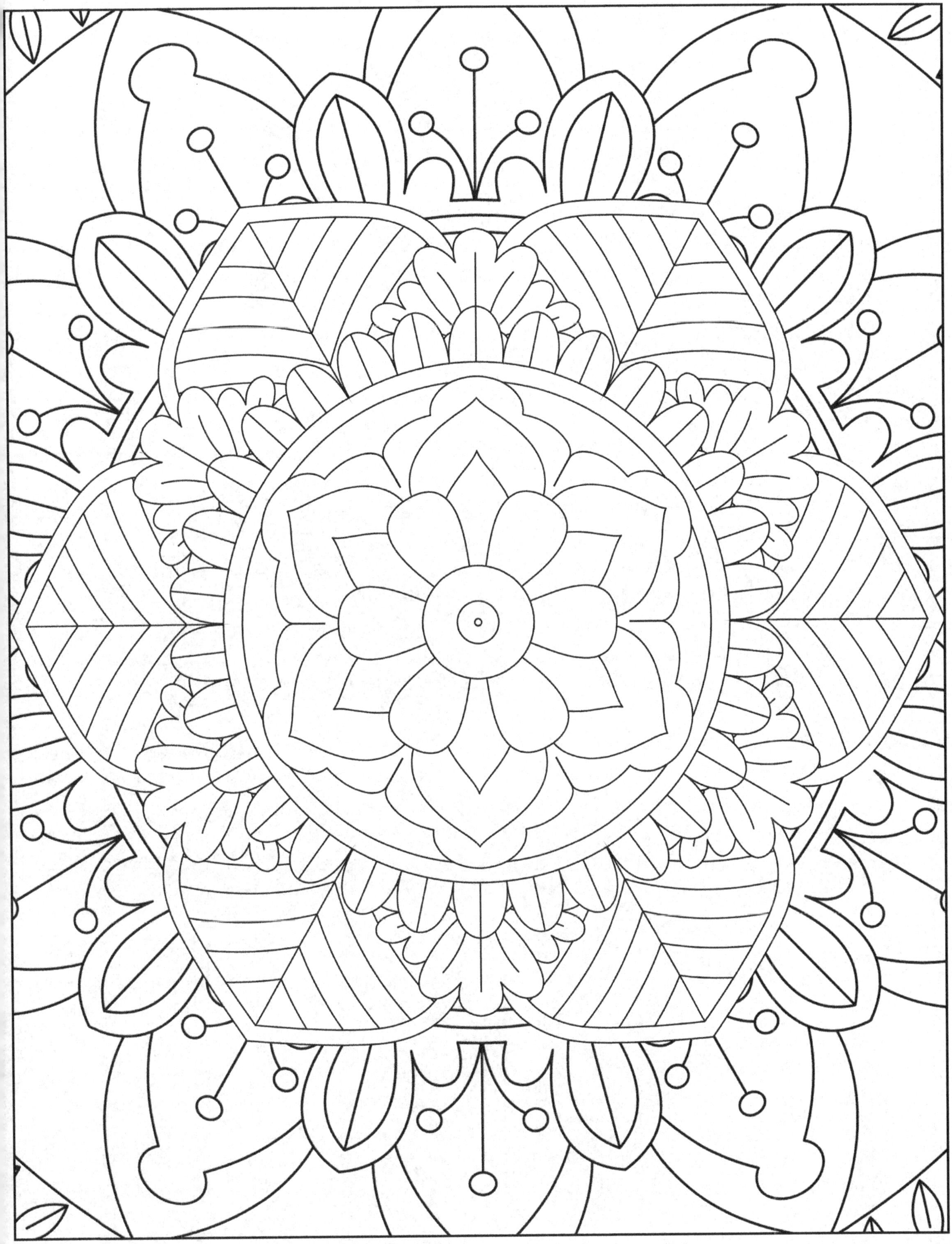

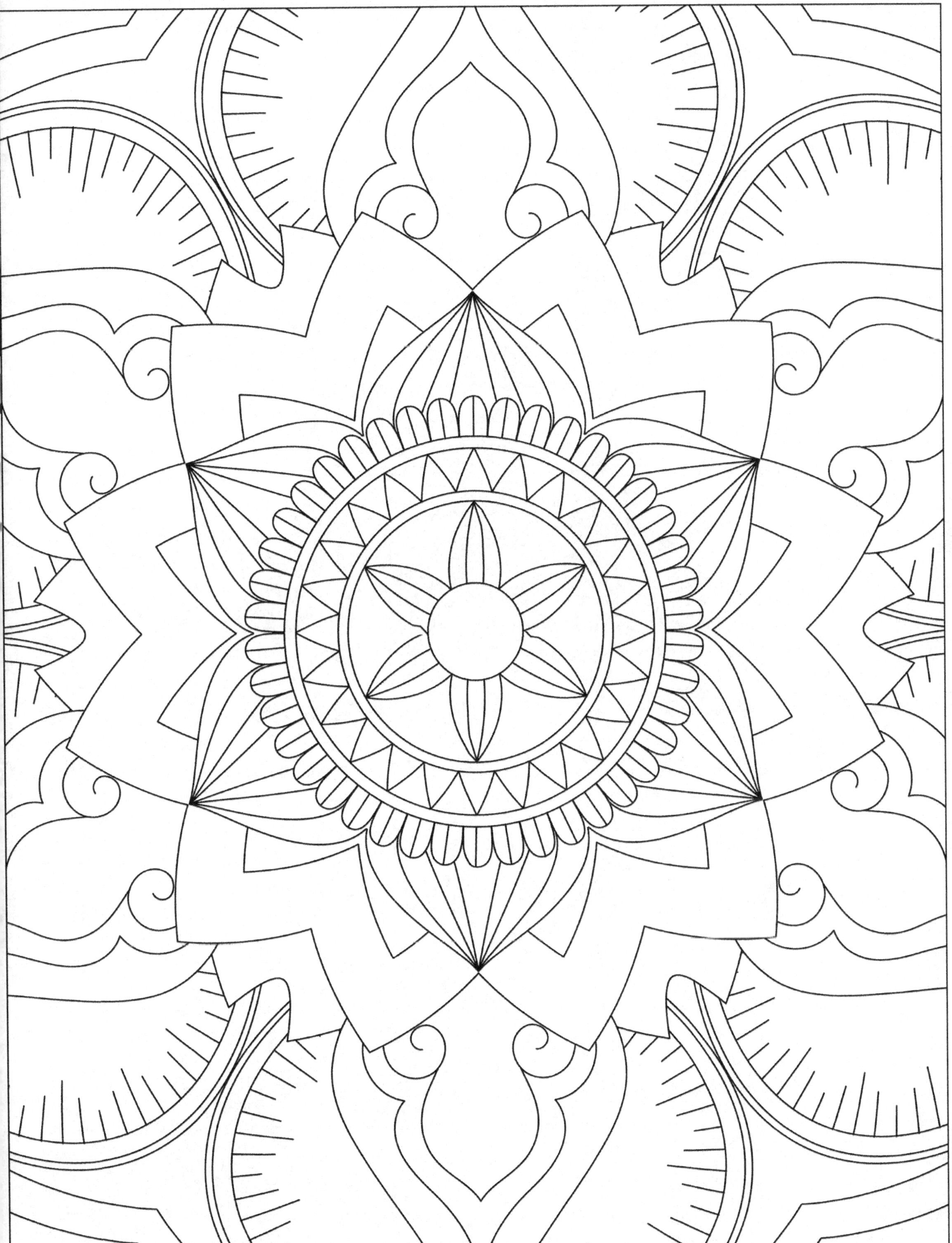

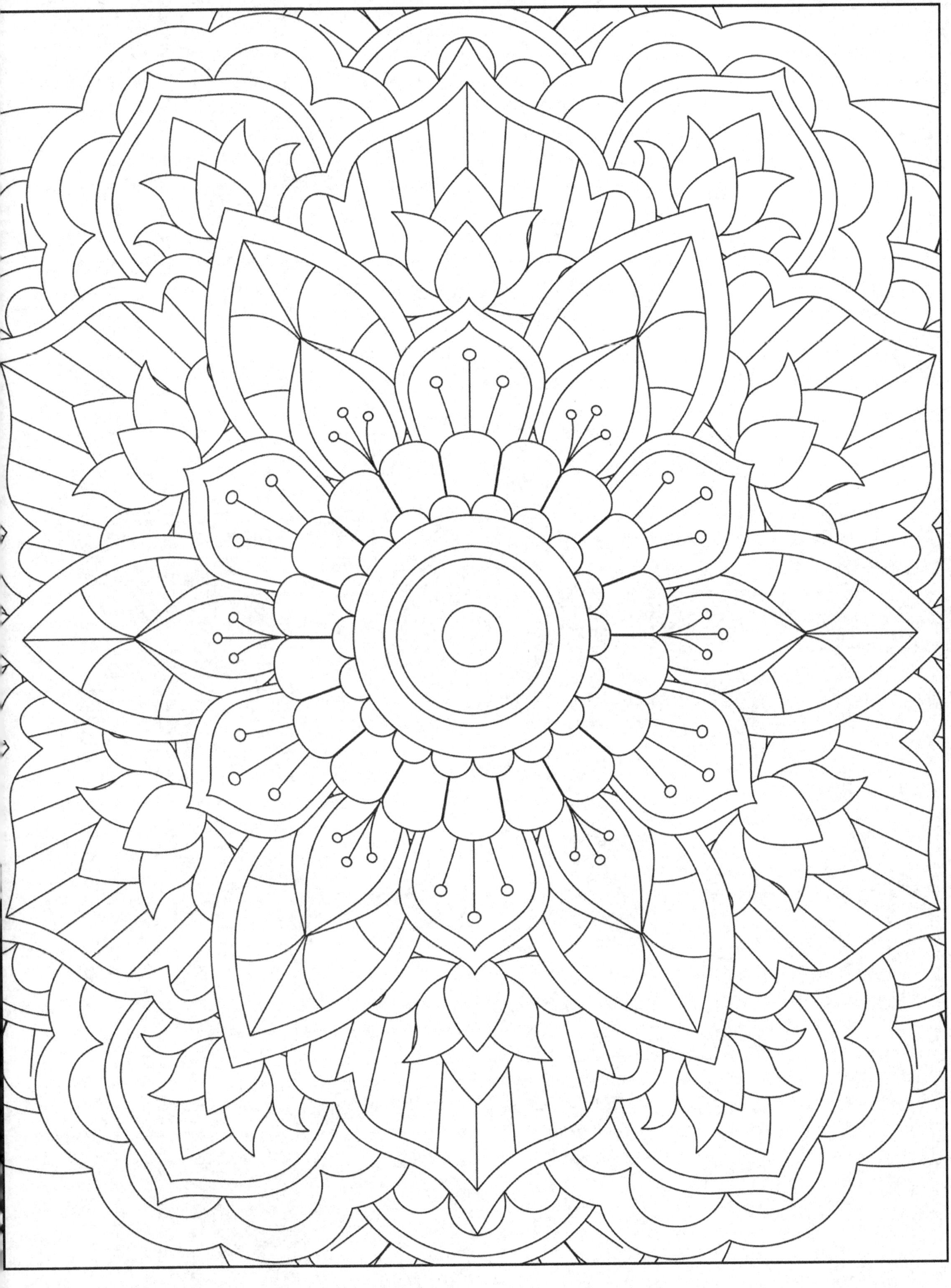

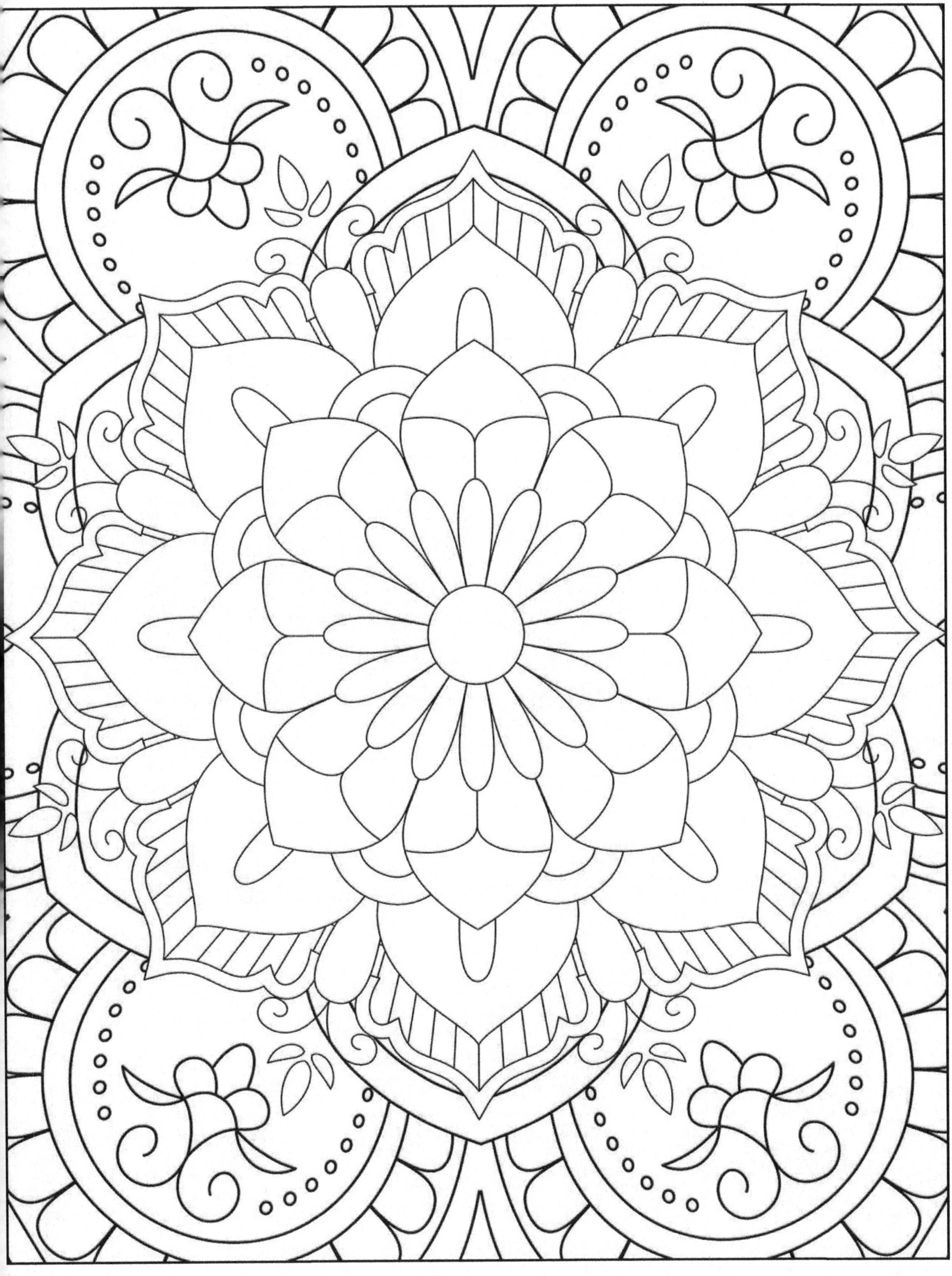

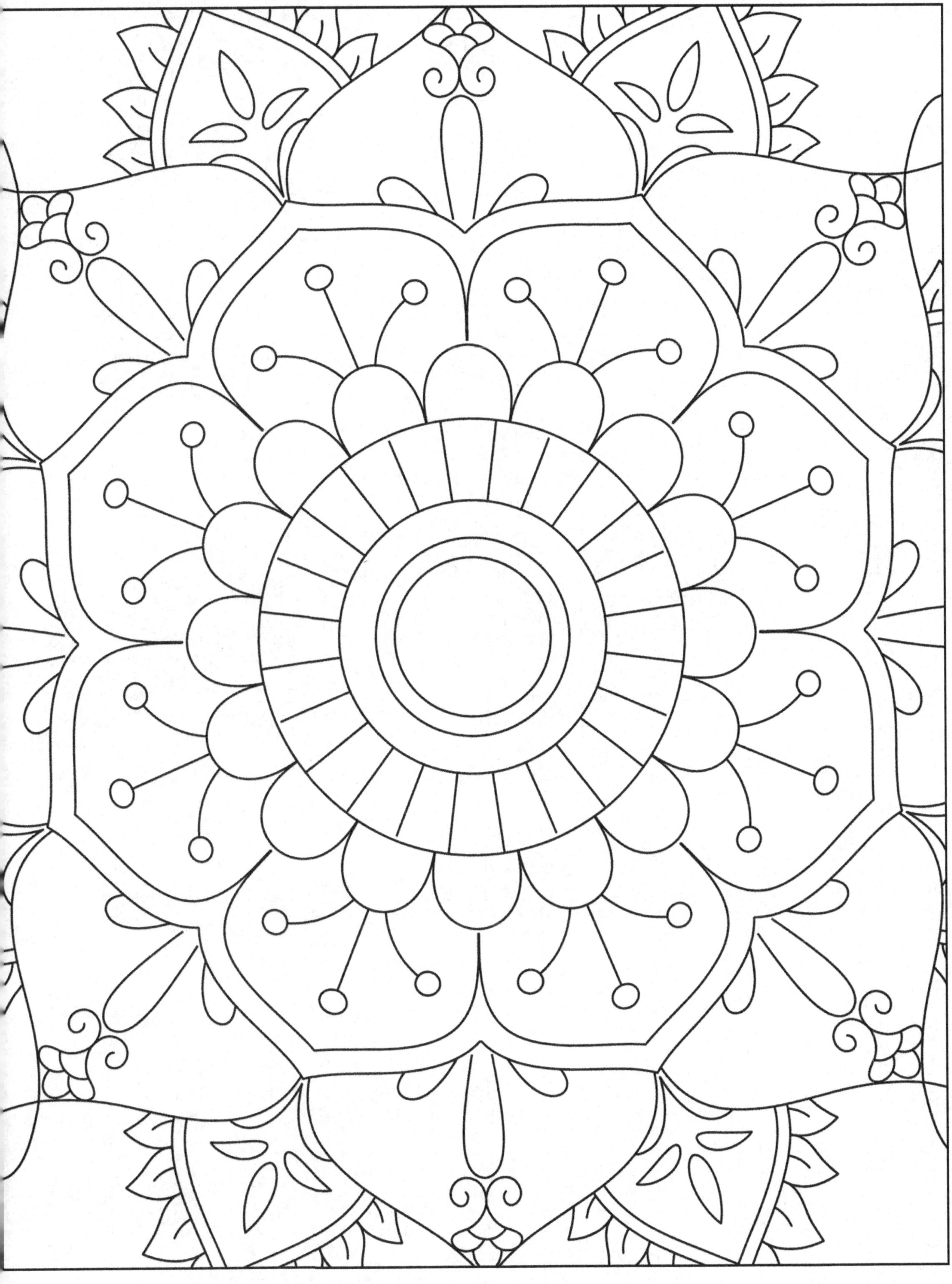

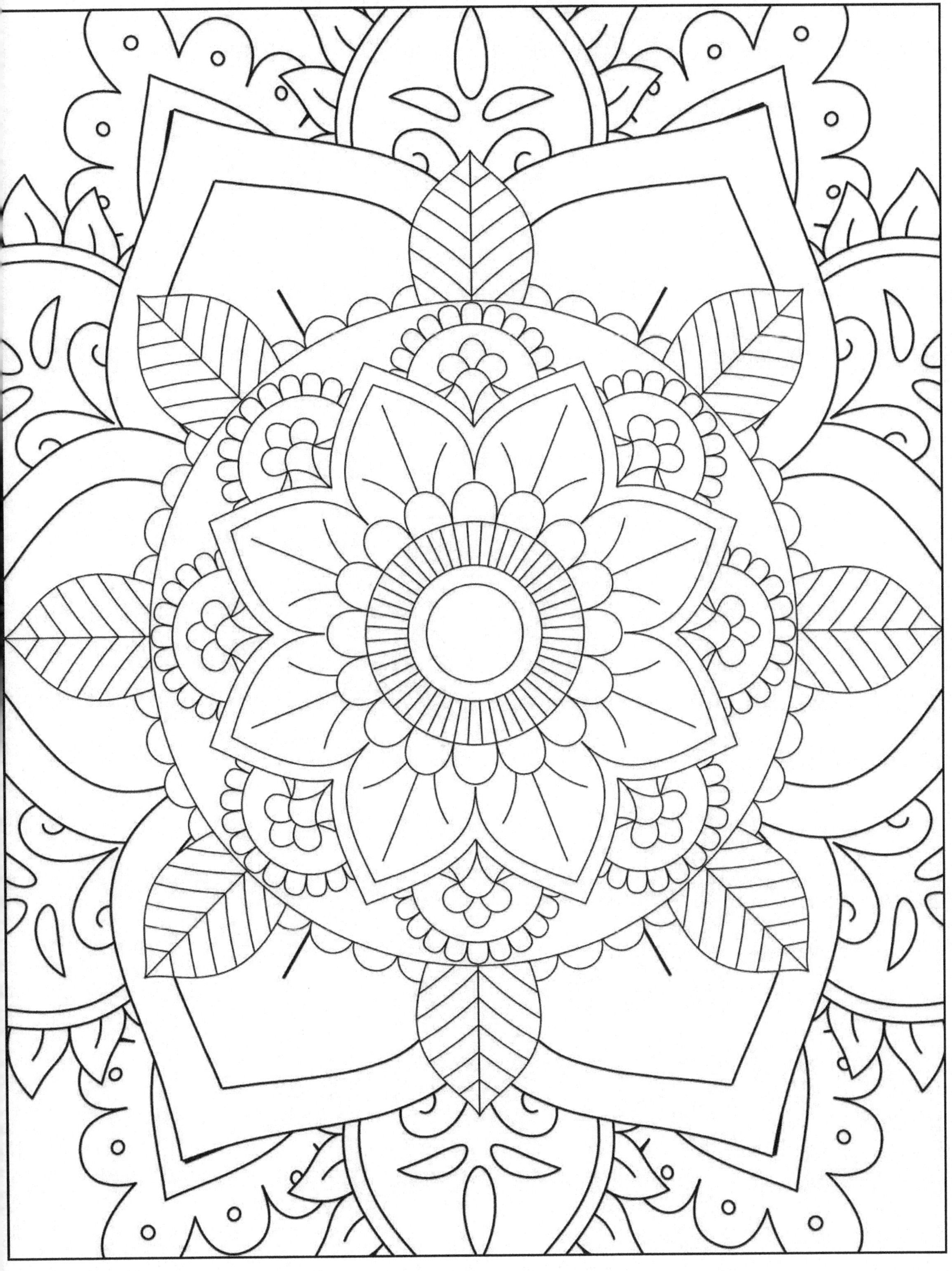

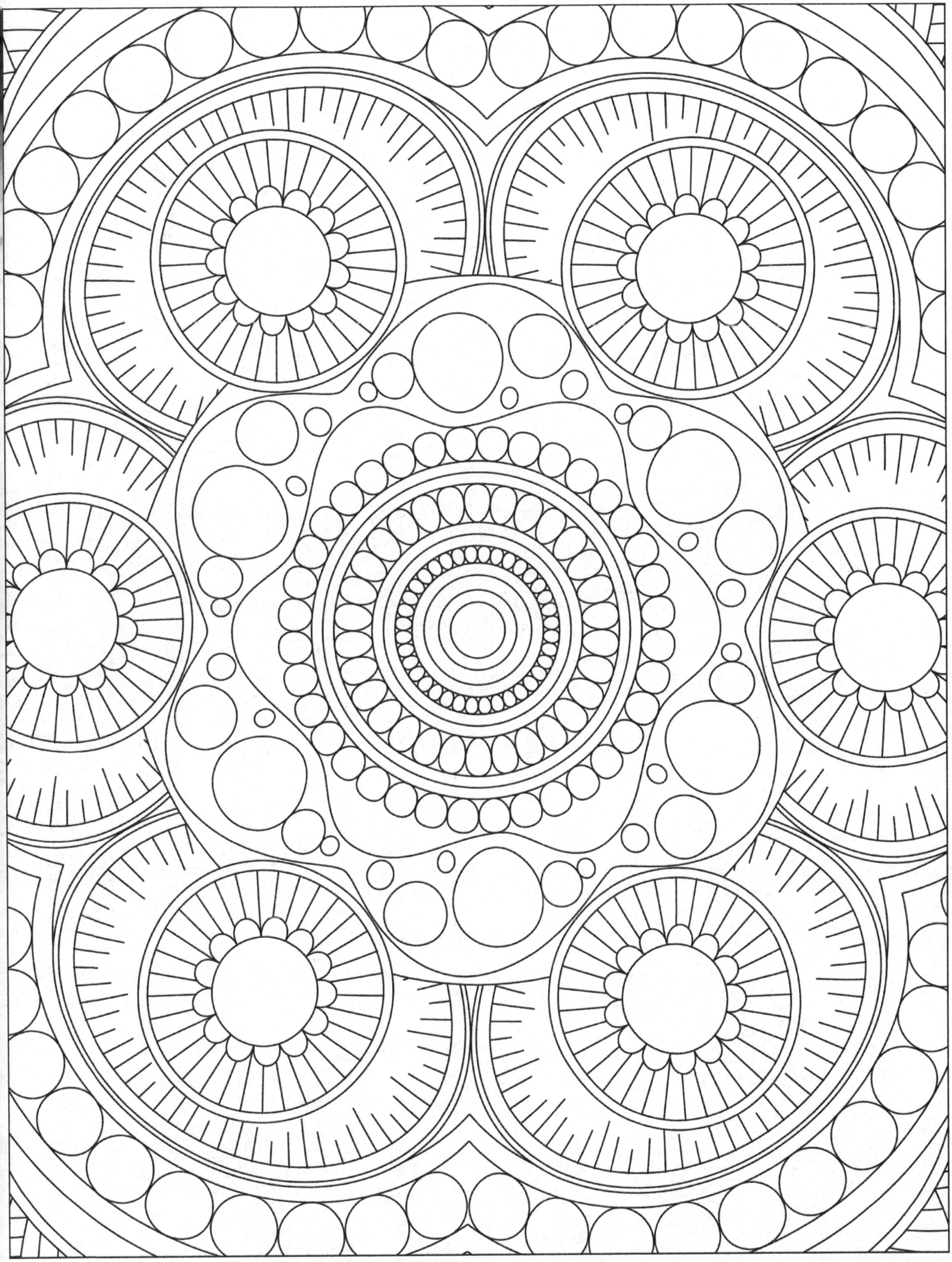

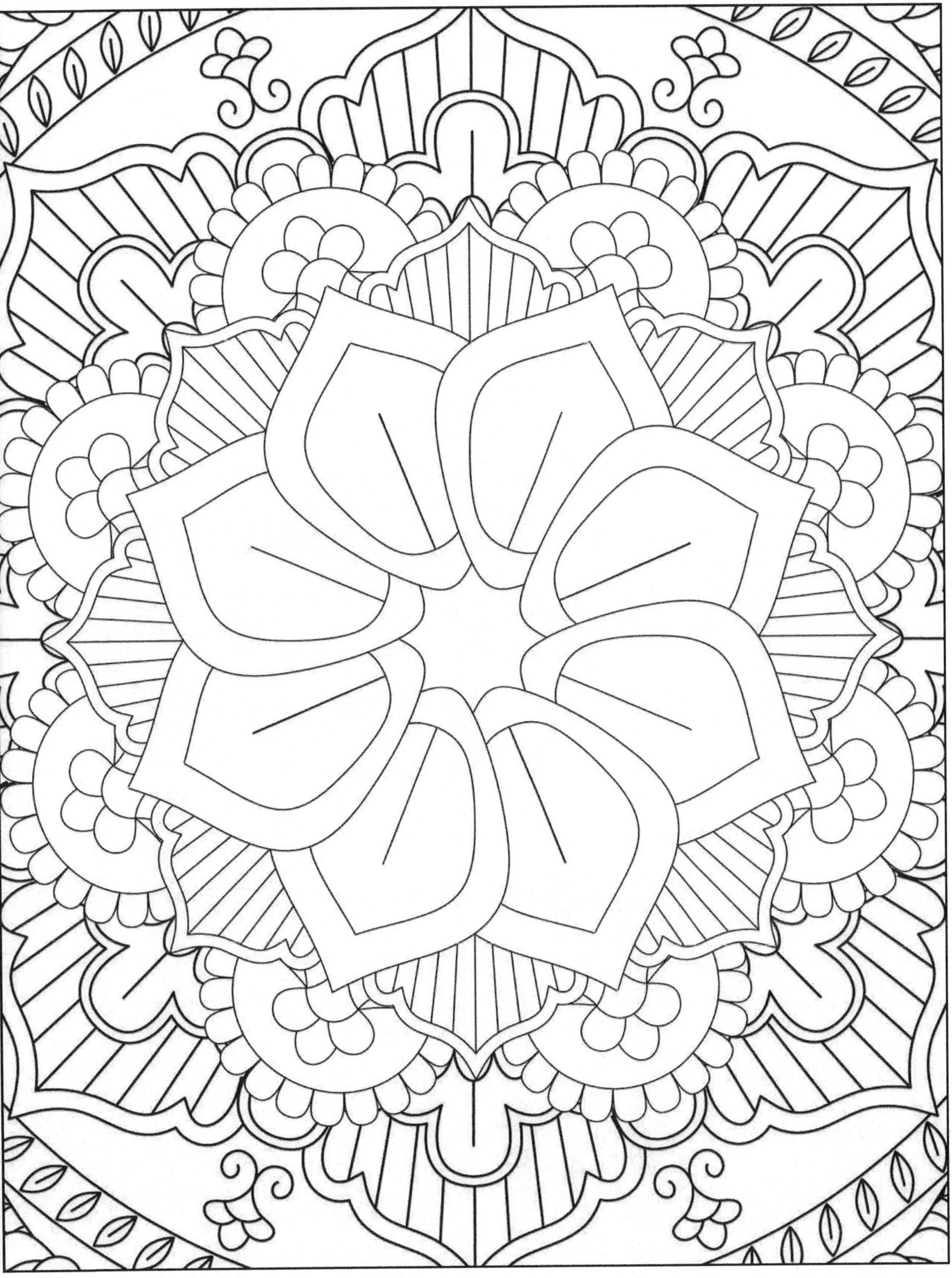

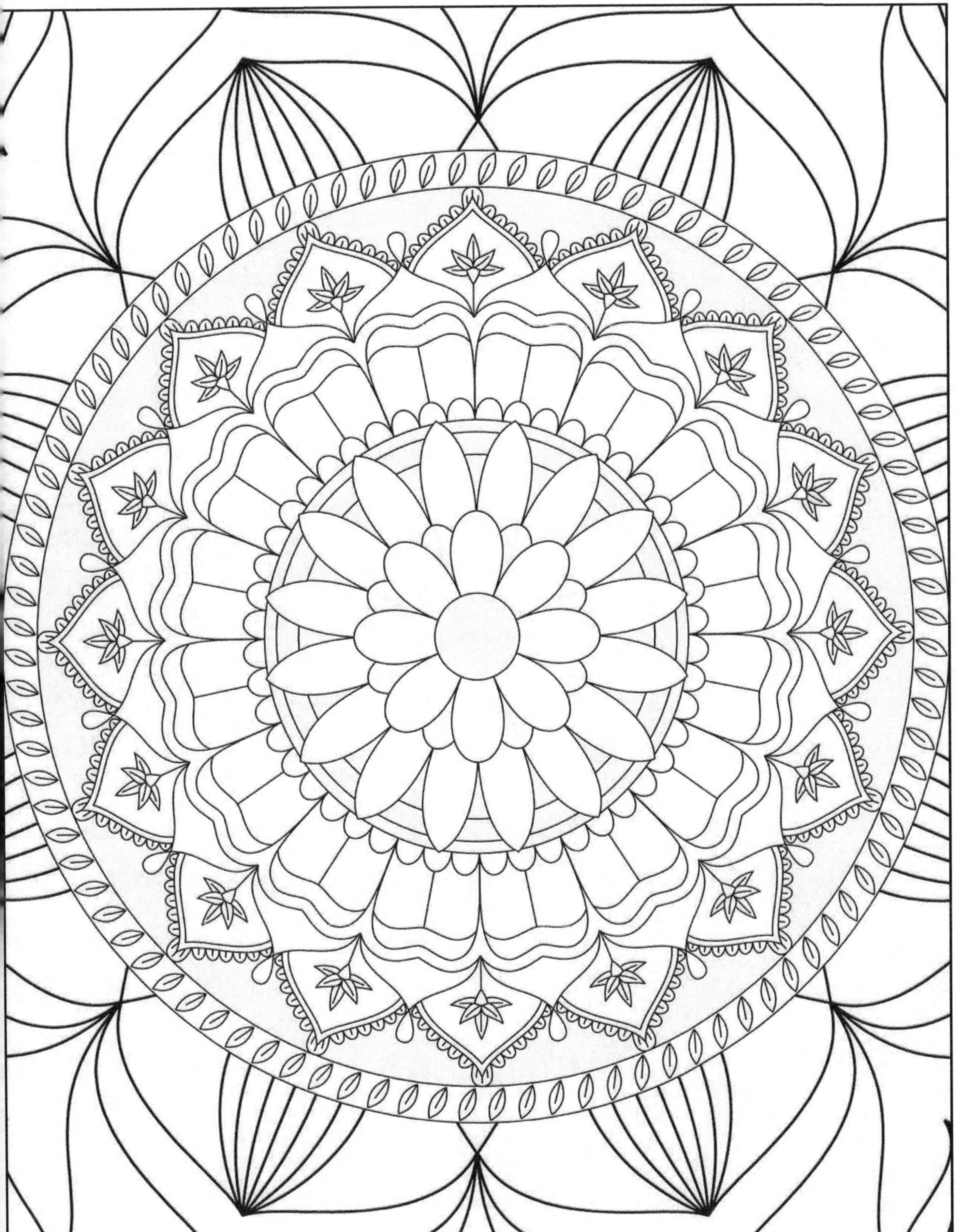

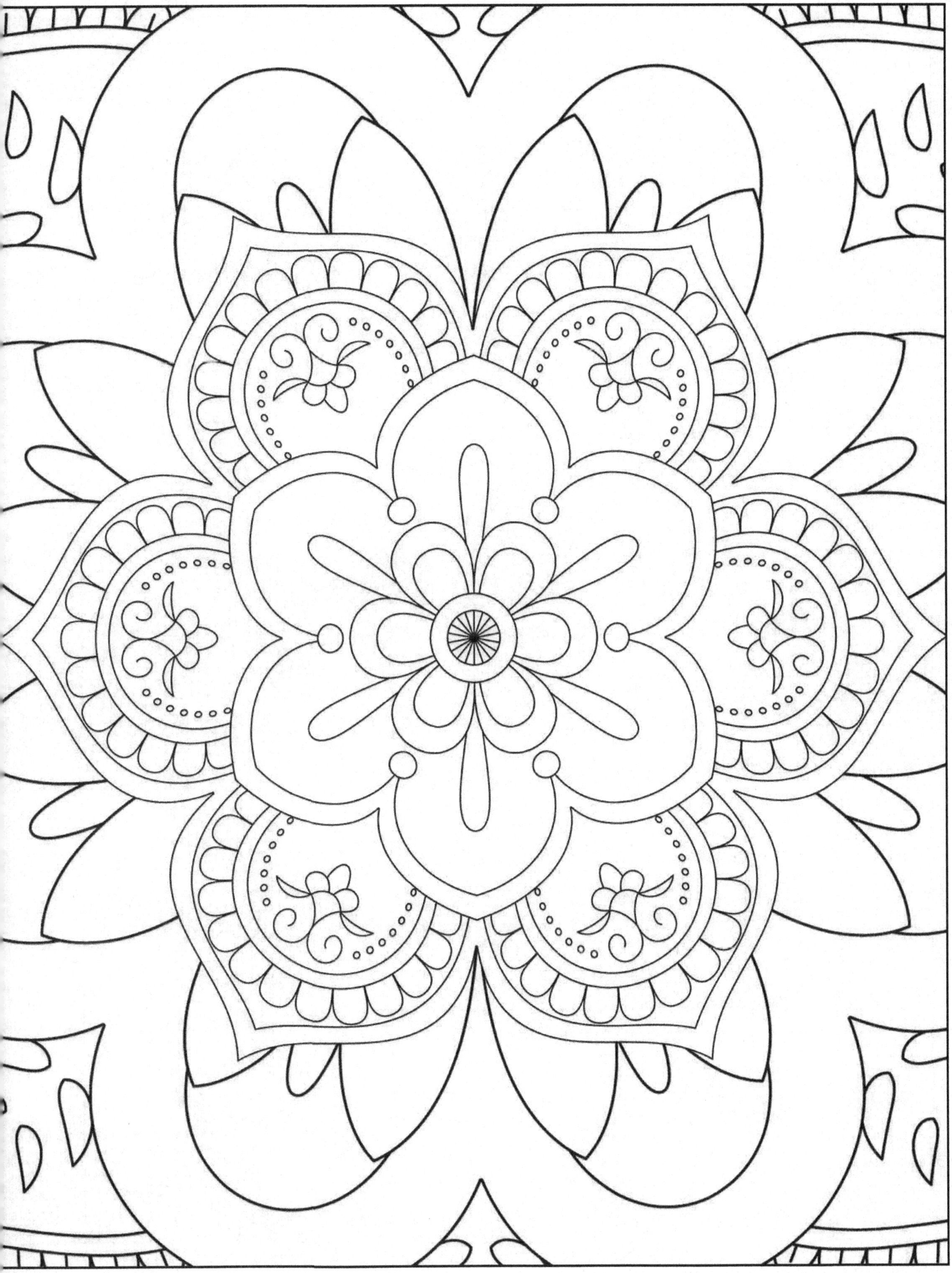

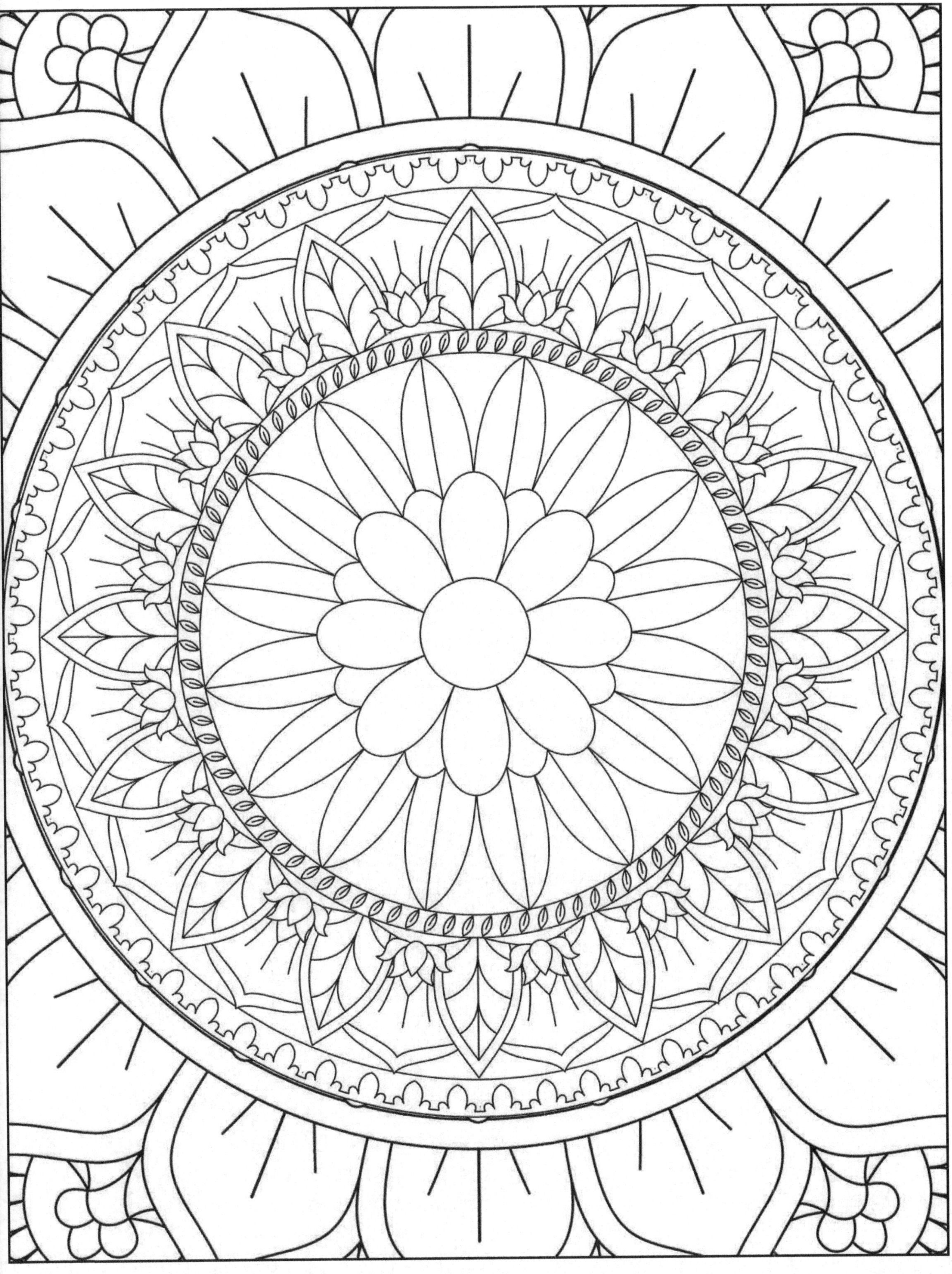

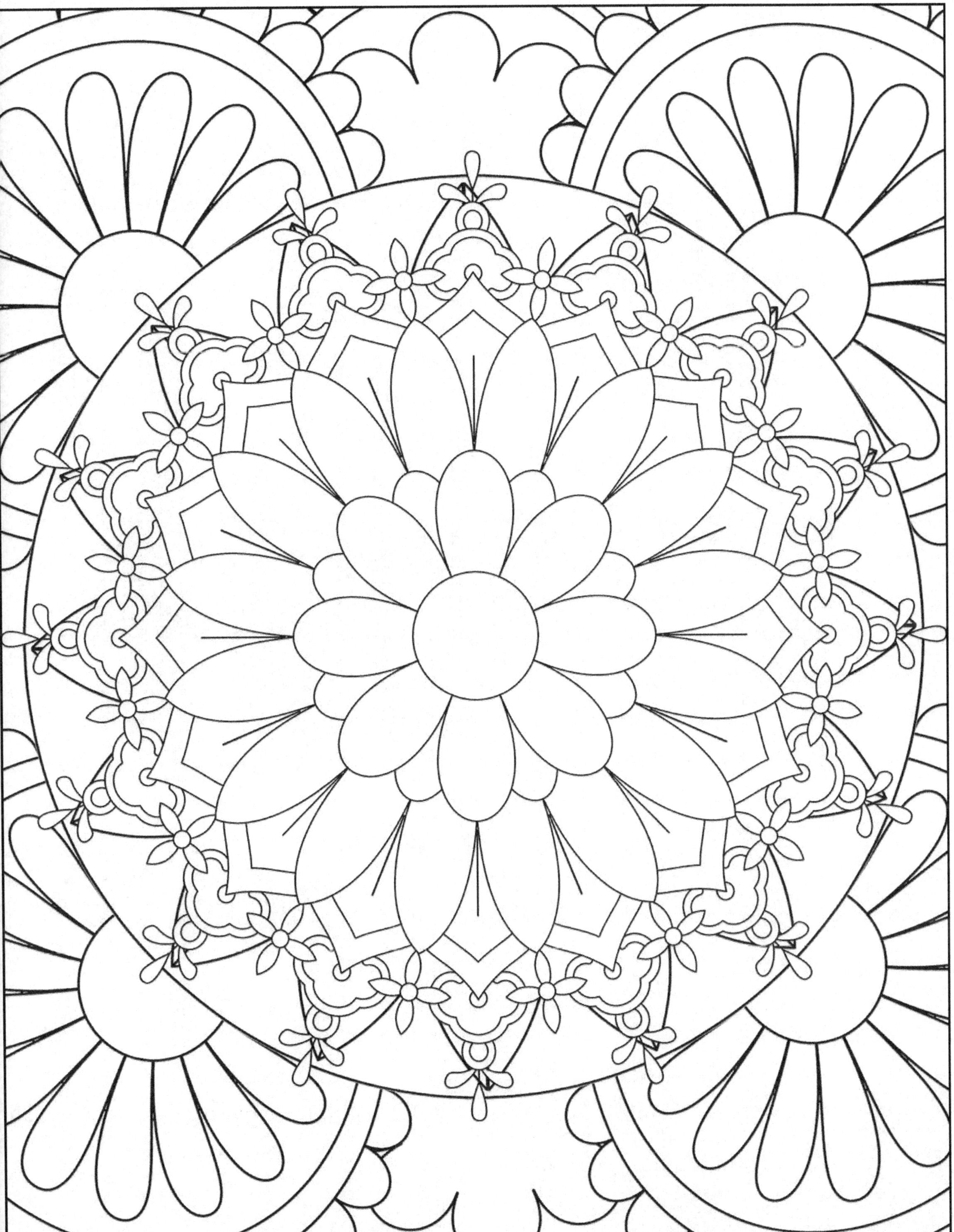

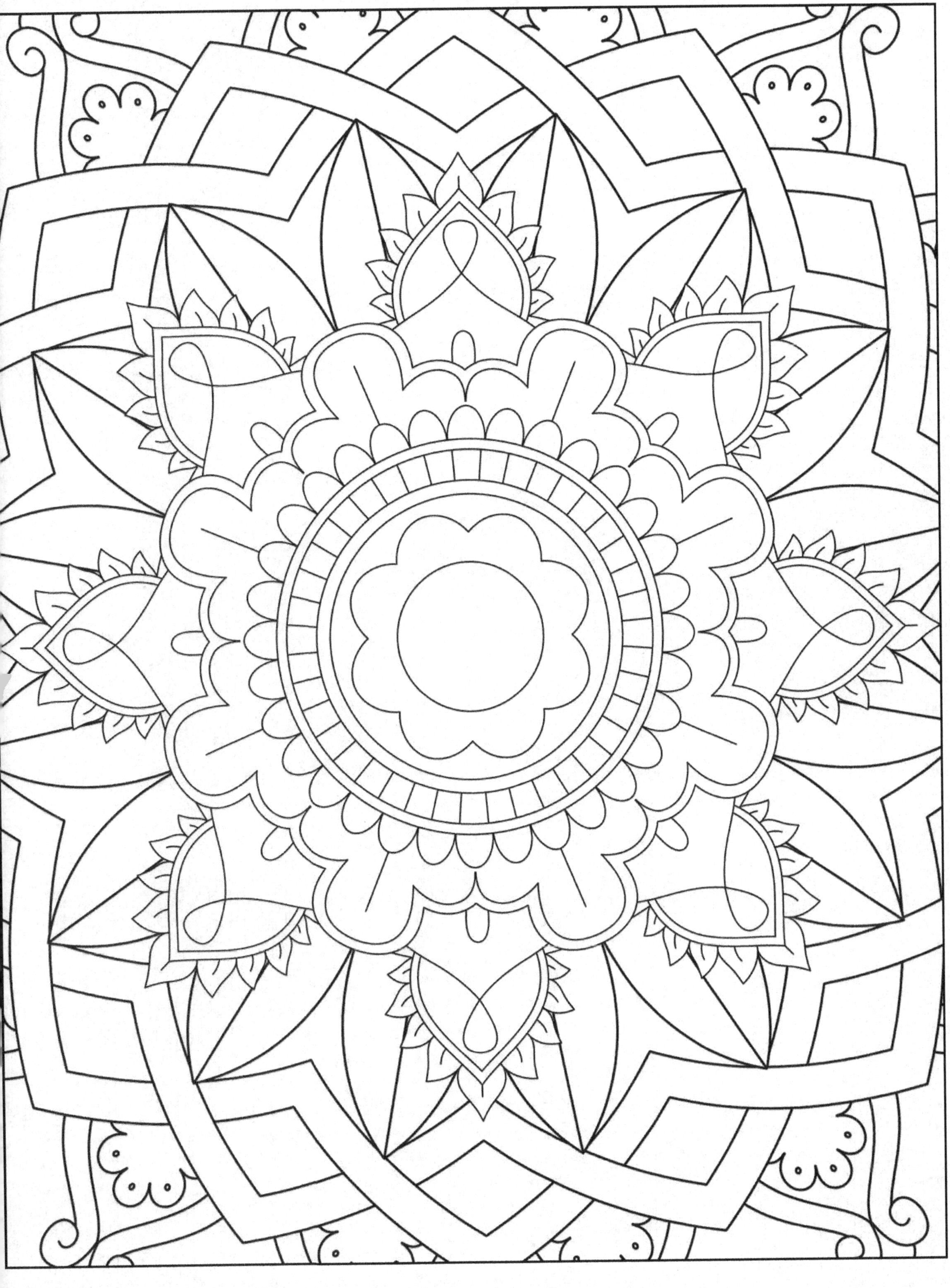

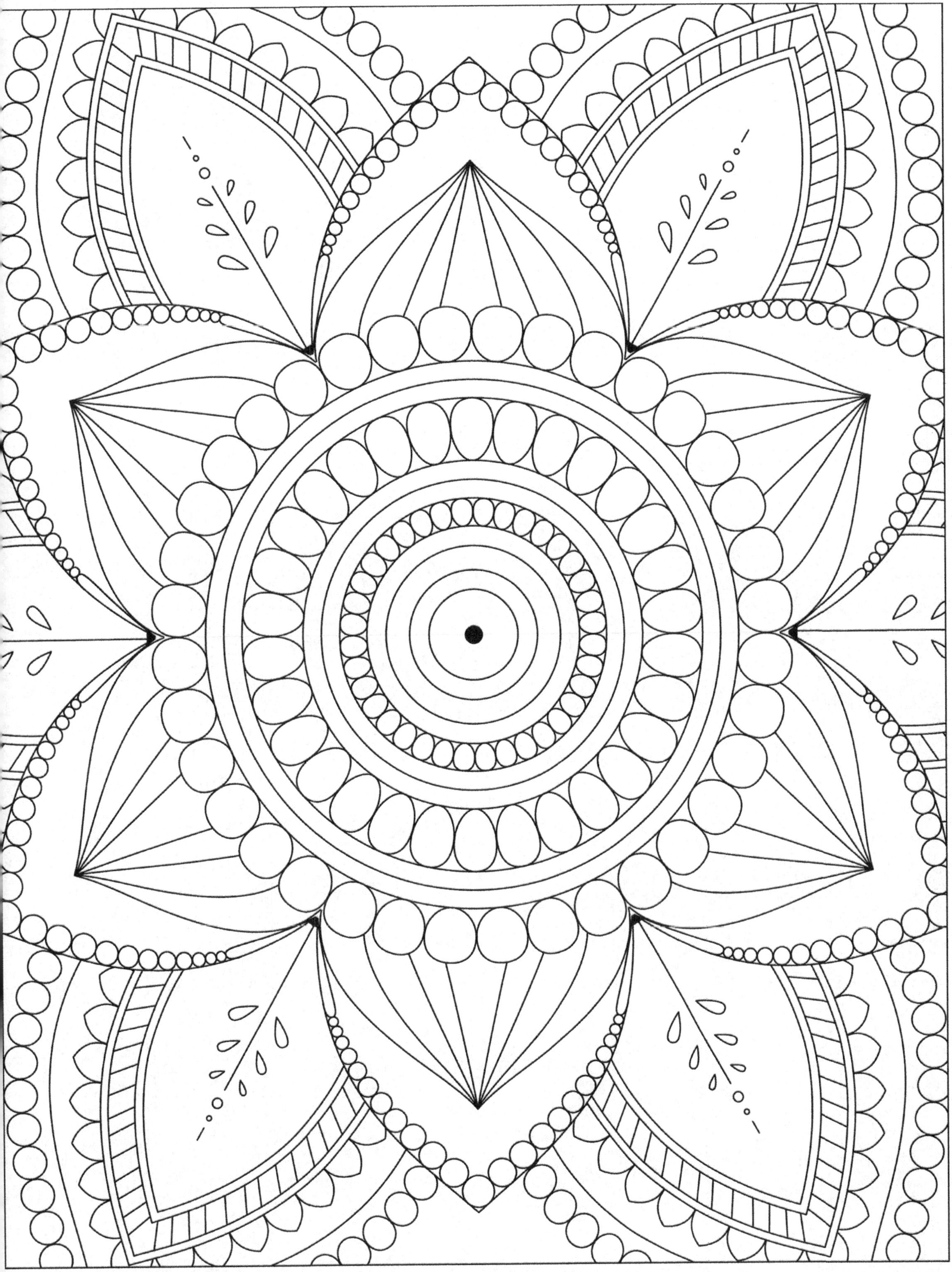

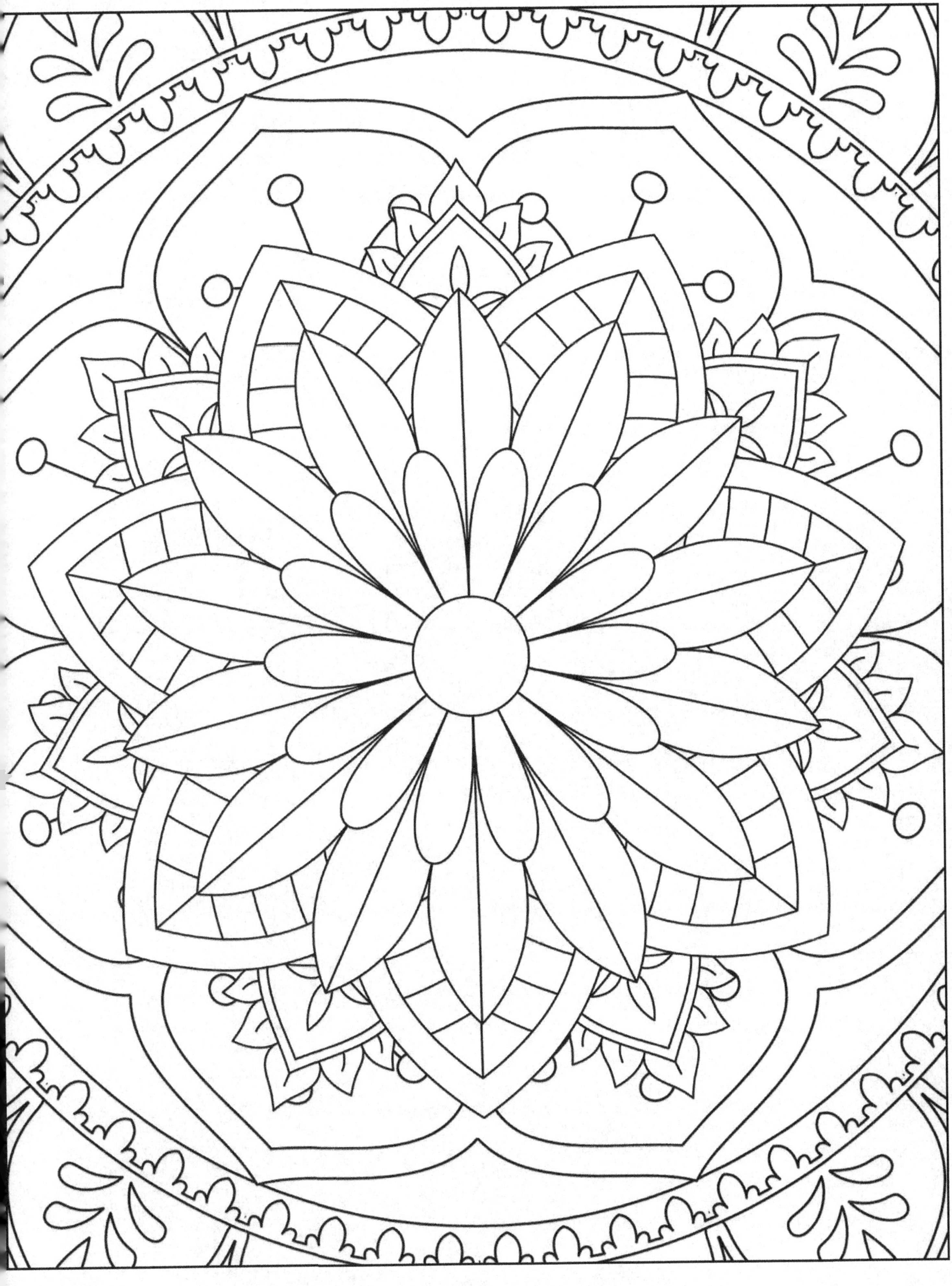

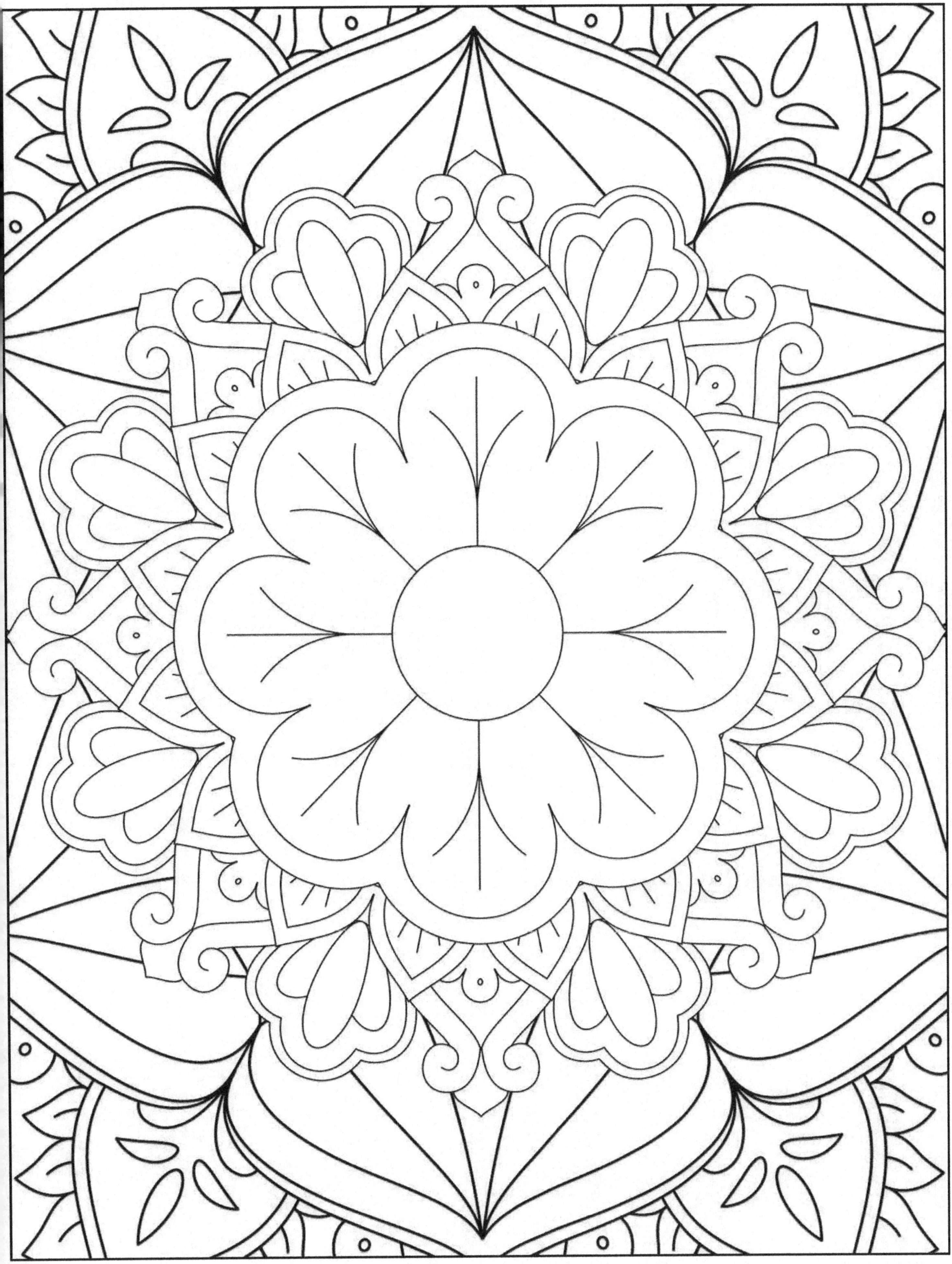

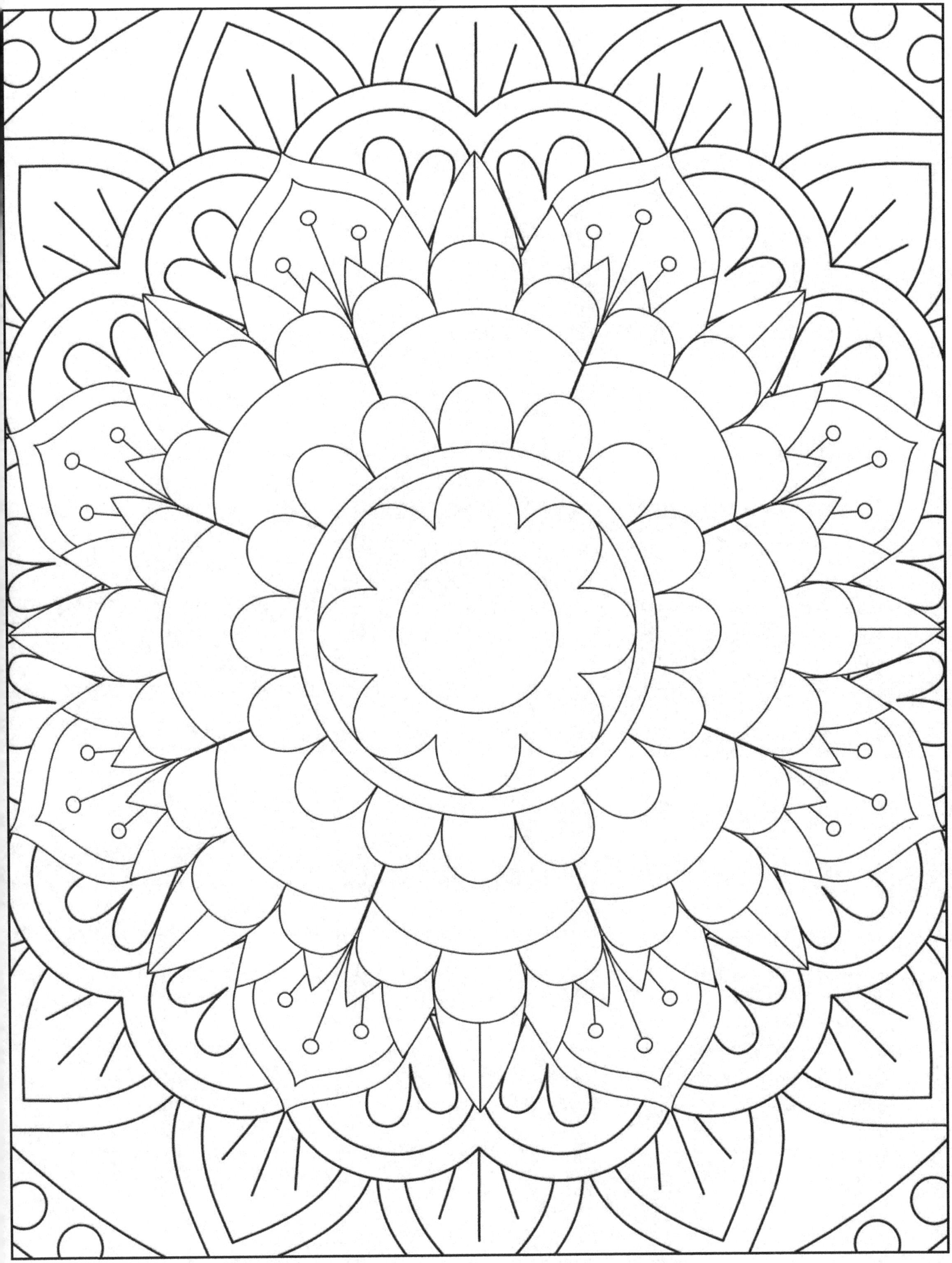

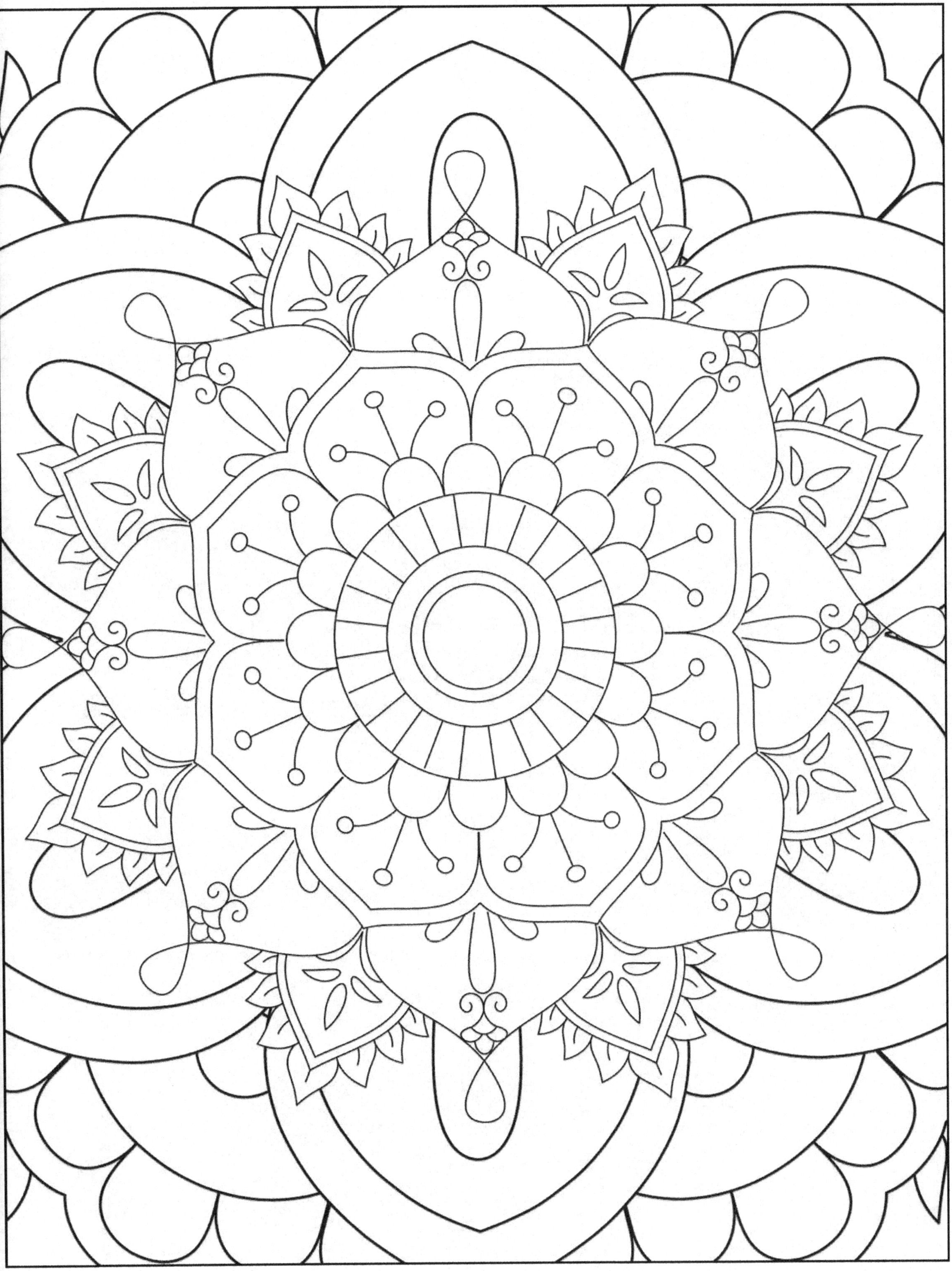

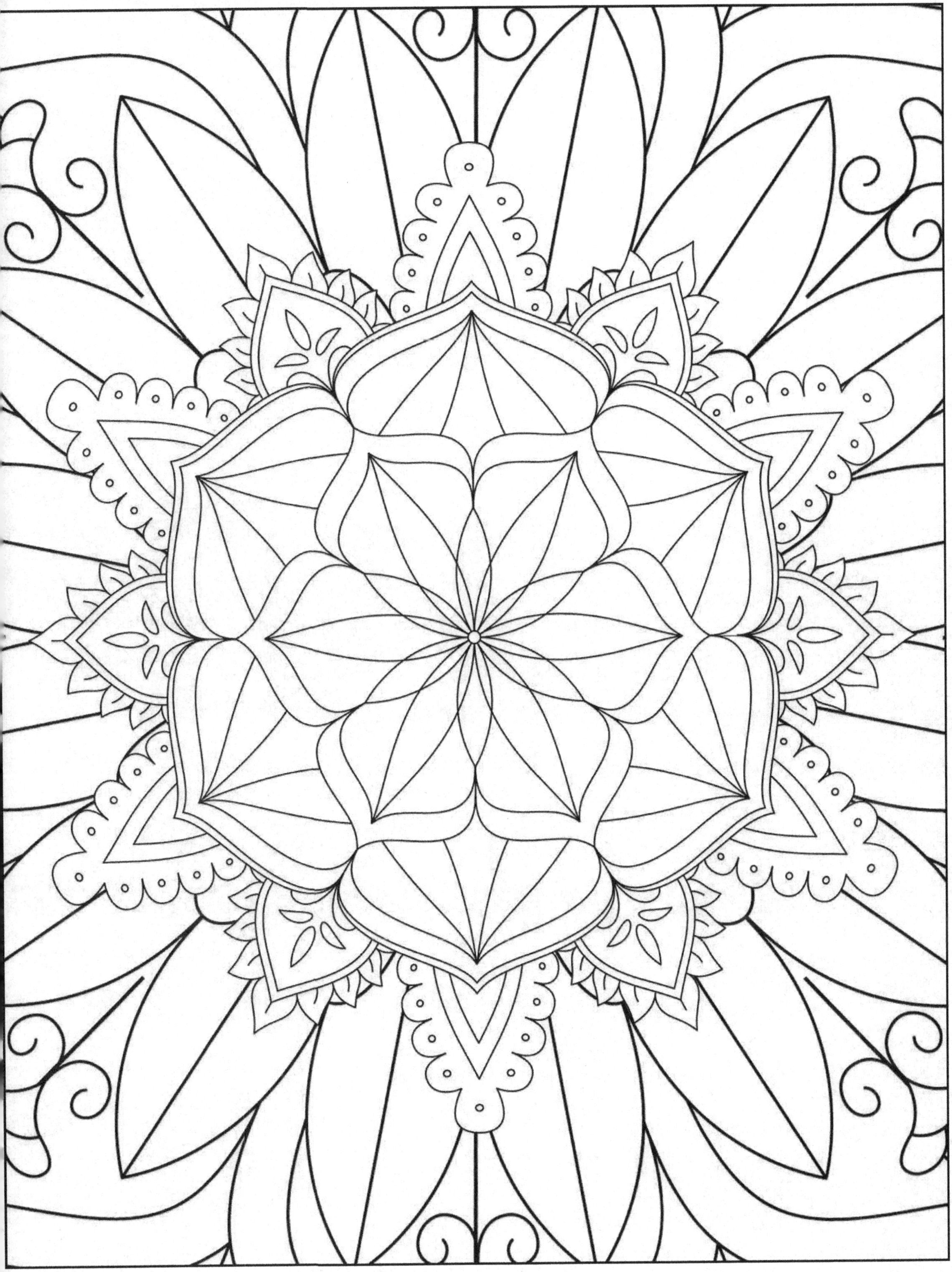

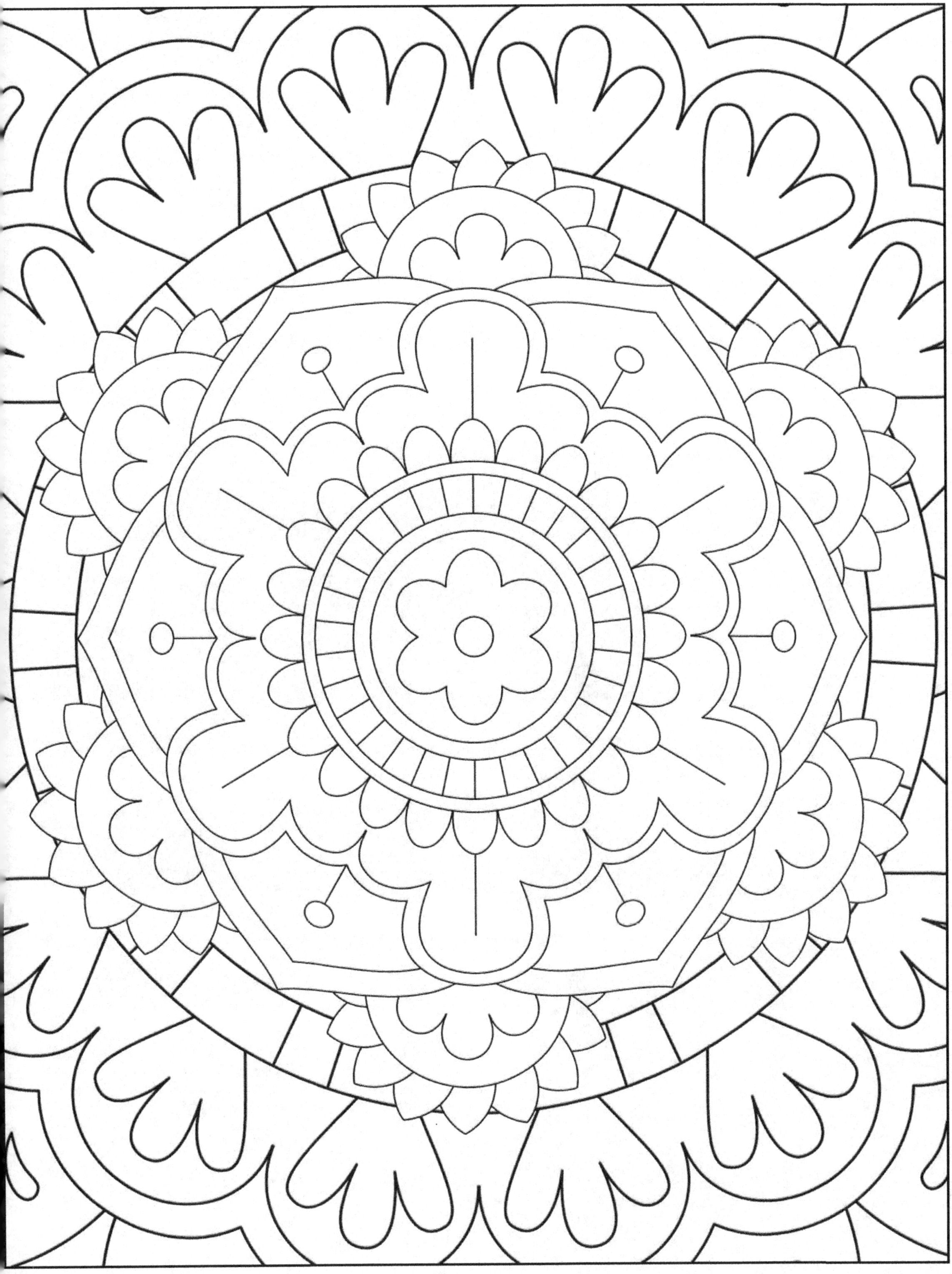

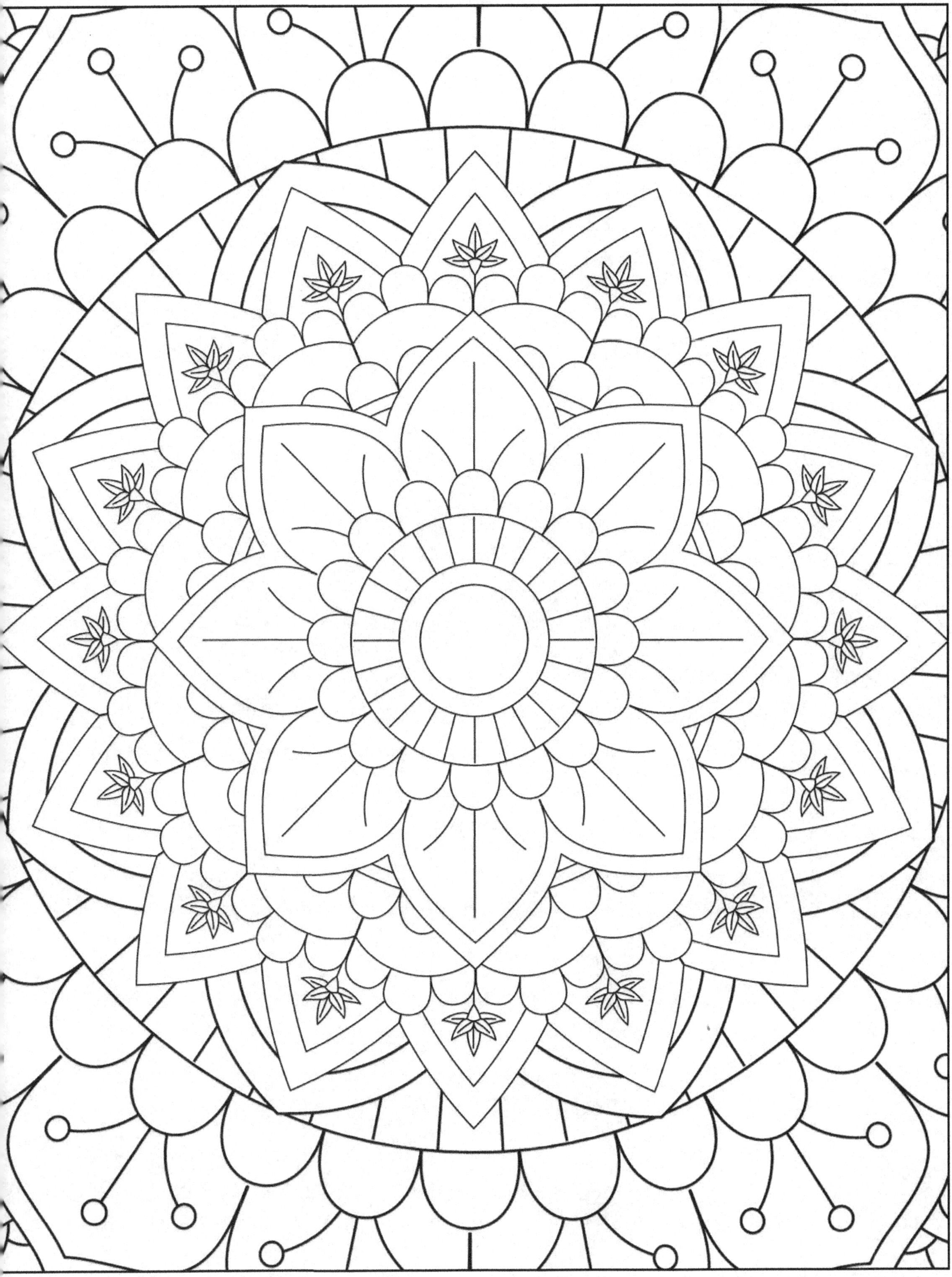

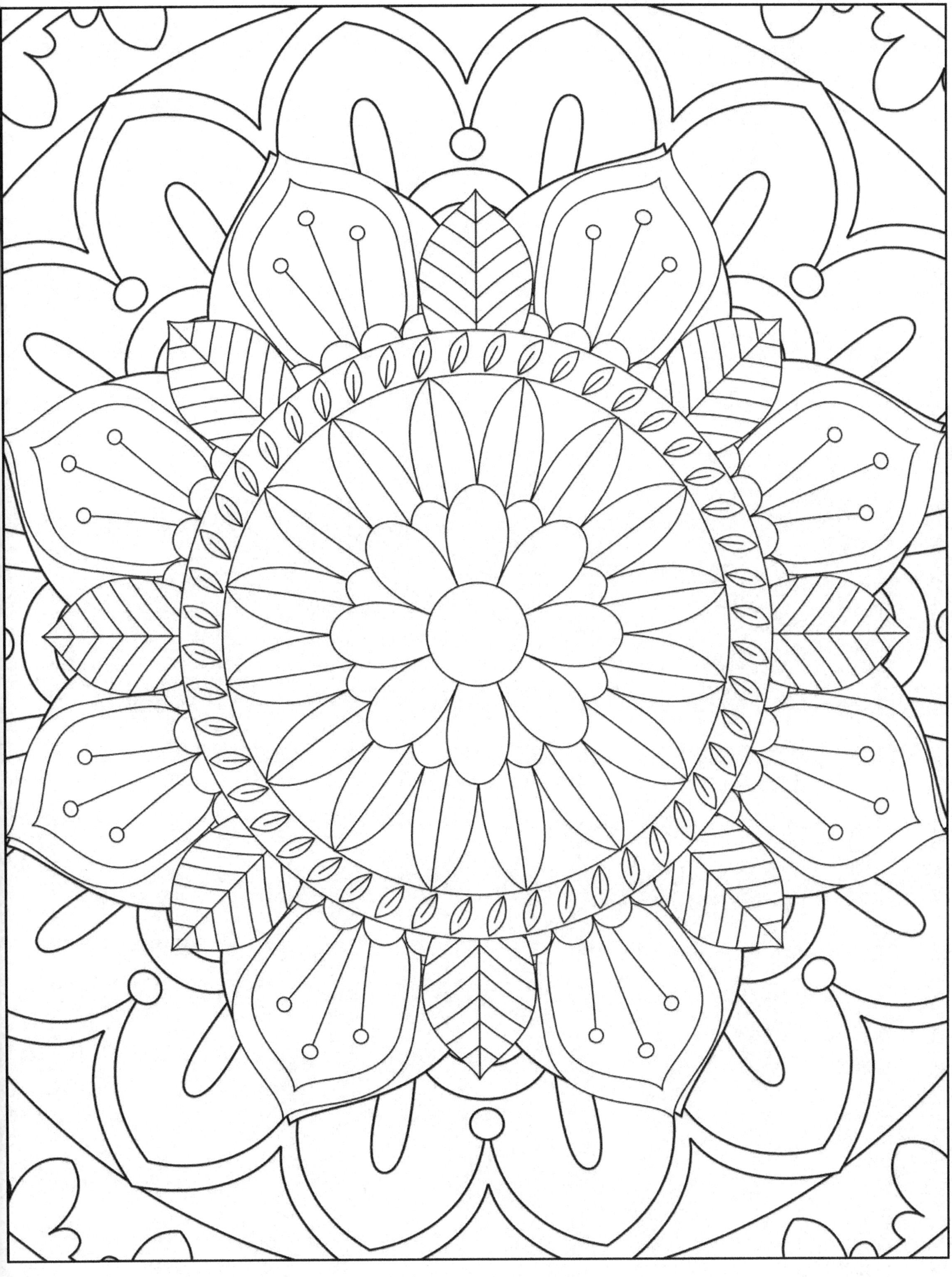

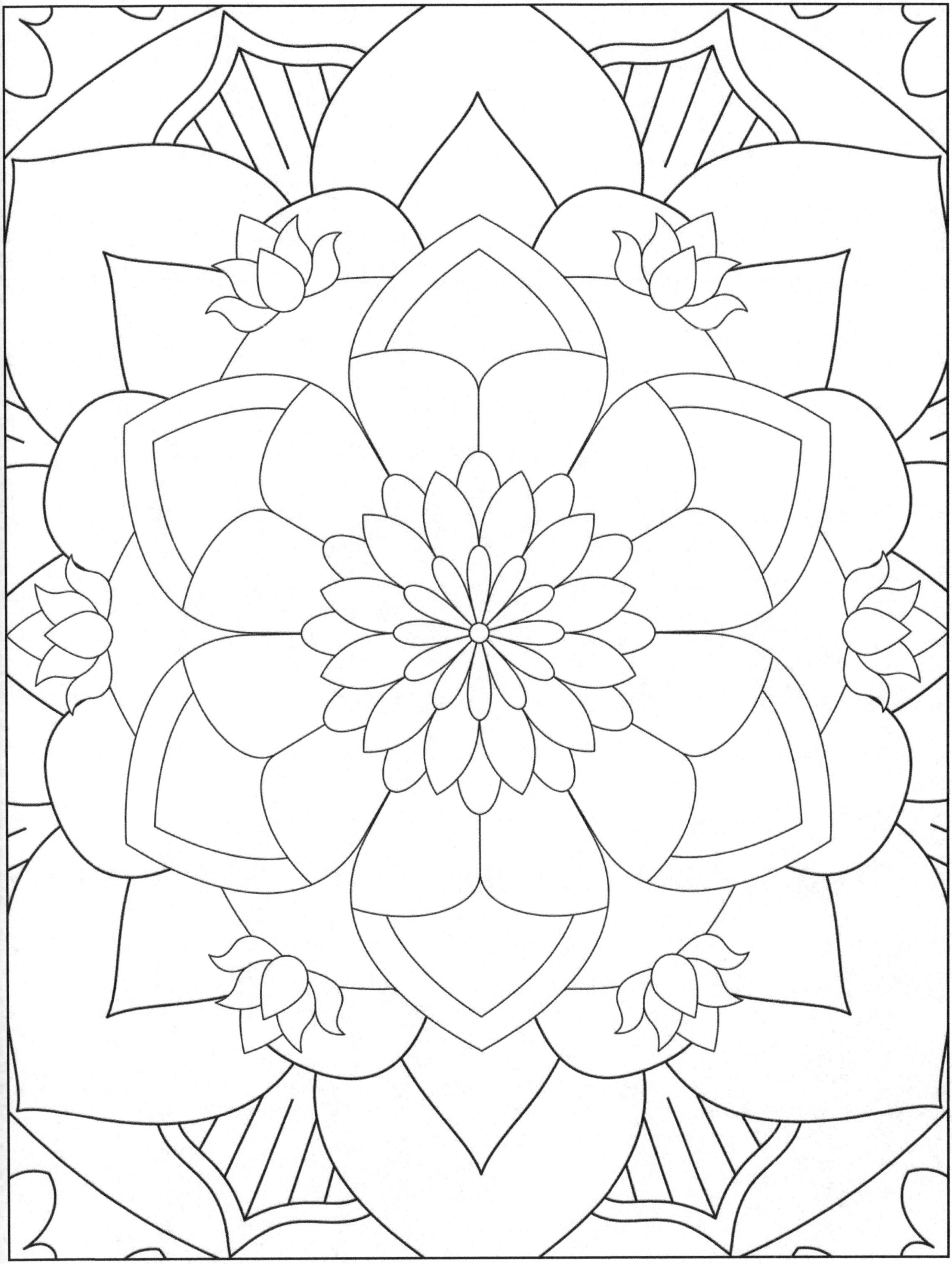

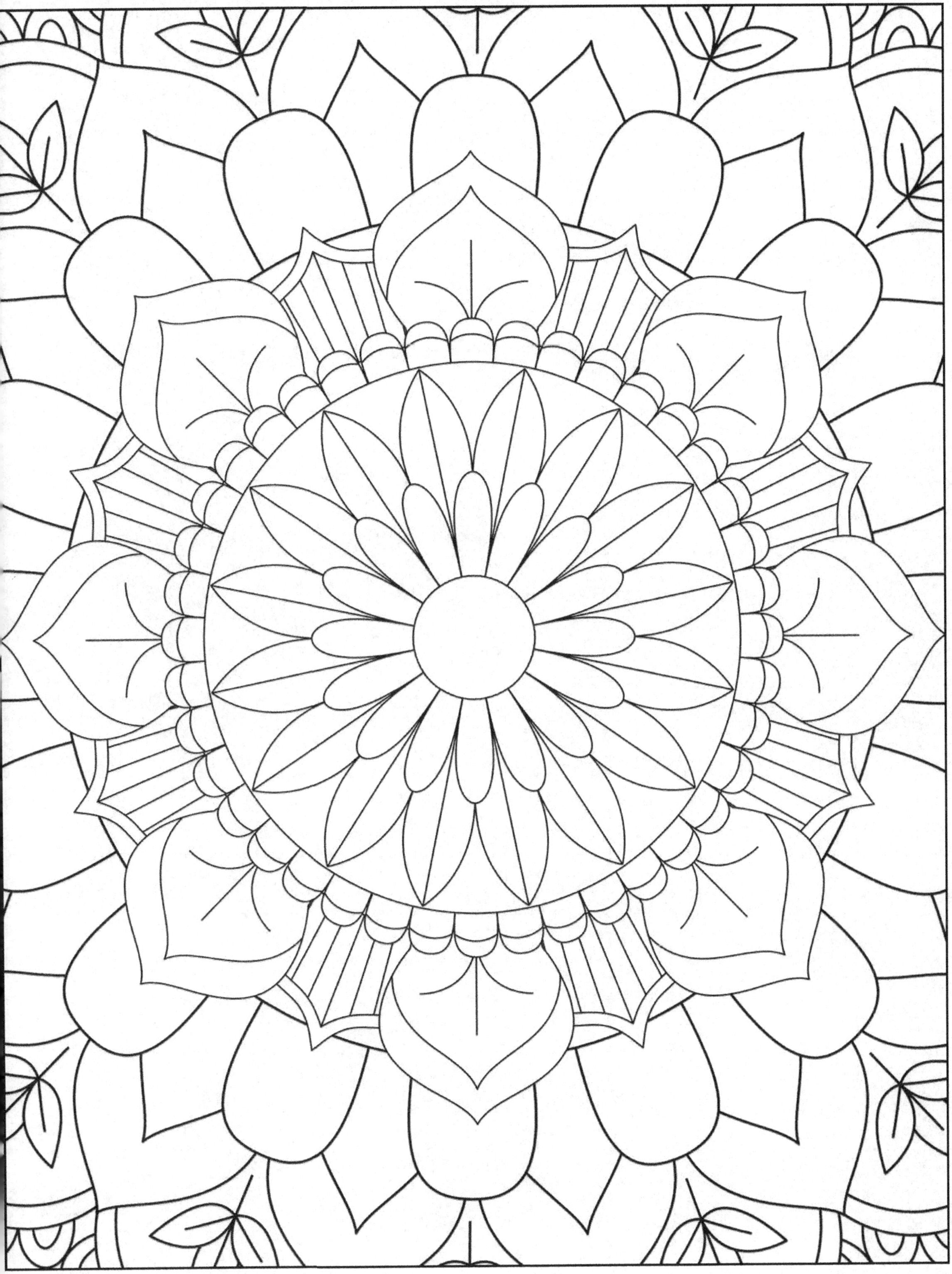

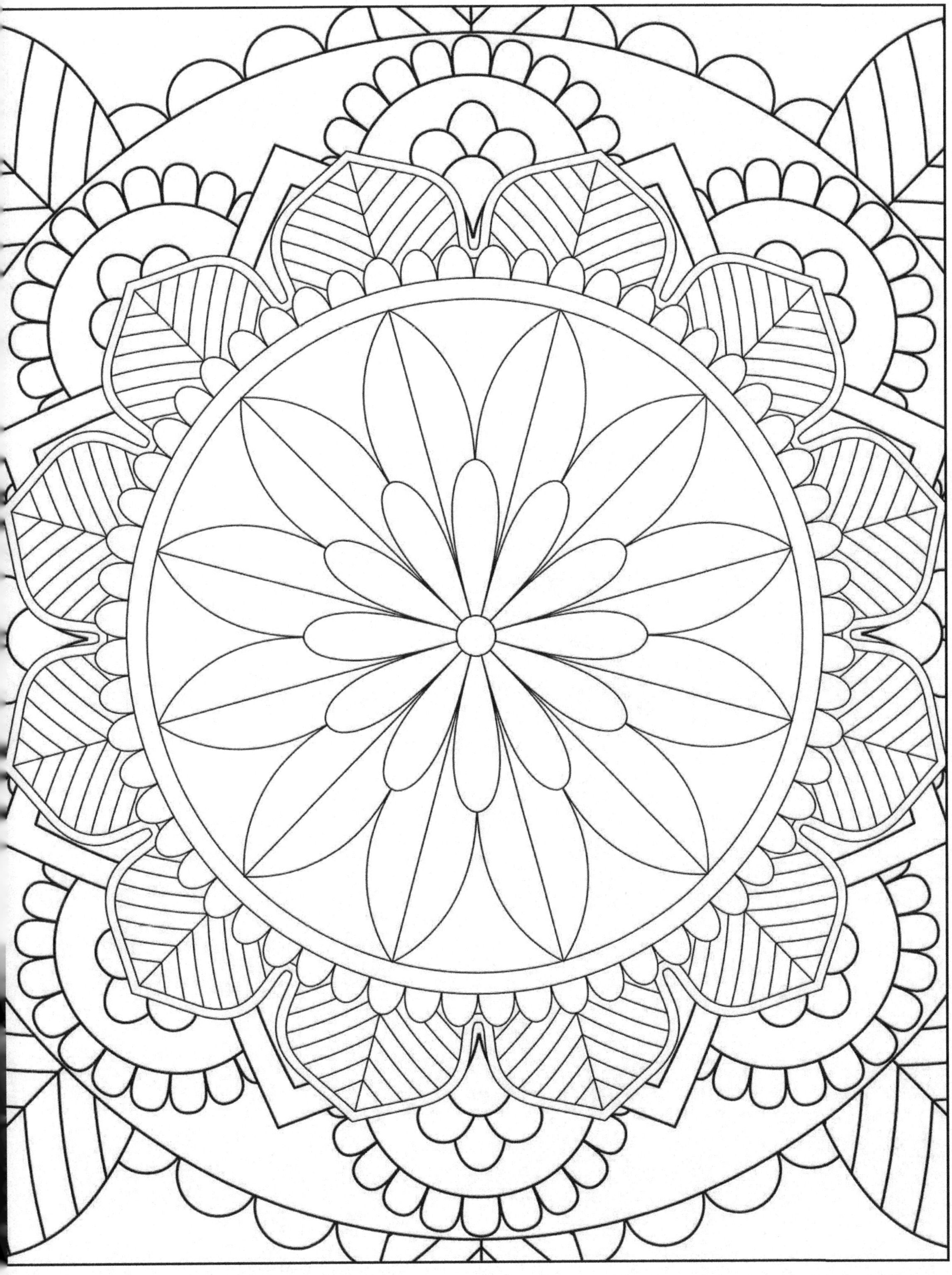

Made in the USA
Middletown, DE
16 October 2023

40944510R00057